Personal Independence Payment
What you need to know

Child Poverty Action Group

Published by Child Poverty Action Group
30 Micawber Street
London N1 7TB
Tel: 020 7837 7979
staff@cpag.org.uk
www.cpag.org.uk
© Child Poverty Action Group 2016

A CIP record for this book is available from the British Library.
ISBN: 978 1 910715 15 4

Child Poverty Action Group is a charity registered in England and Wales (registration number 294841) and in Scotland (registration number SC039339), and is a company limited by guarantee, registered in England (registration number 1993854). VAT number: 690 808117

Cover design by Colorido Studios
Typeset by David Lewis XML Associates Ltd
Content management system by KonnectSoft
Printed and bound in the UK by CPI Group (UK) Ltd

Author
Jon Shaw is a welfare rights worker at CPAG in Scotland.

Acknowledgements
Many thanks are due to the authors of the first edition: Edward Graham, Nick Jones
and David Simmons. For assissting with this edition, thank you to Barabara Donegan,
Alison Lord, David Simmons and Mark Willis. Thanks also to Nicola Johnston for
editing and managing the production of this book, Katherine Dawson for compiling the
index and Pauline Phillips for proofreading the text.

About Child Poverty Action Group

Child Poverty Action Group is a national charity working for the abolition of child poverty in the UK and for the improvement of the lives of low-income families.

To help achieve this goal, we have developed a high level of expertise in the welfare benefits system. We use this to support thousands of advisers with our expert training and free helplines, enabling them to give families the best information and advice.

We also publish a widely used series of practitioner handbooks – our annual *Welfare Benefits and Tax Credits Handbook* (known as 'the adviser's bible') is used by citizens advice bureaux, local authorities and law centres throughout the UK.

Our policy, campaigning and lobbying work builds support for policy improvements to help children living in poverty. We host the End Child Poverty campaign, a national coalition of charities, faith groups and other organisations working to hold the government to its target of beating child poverty by 2020.

If you would like to help us to end child poverty, please visit www.cpag.org.uk. or follow us on Facebook (www.facebook.com/cpaguk) and Twitter @CPAGUK.

Keeping up to date

Advisers can get the latest information on personal independence payment by booking on a CPAG training course. We also provide in-house training. See www.cpag.org.uk/training for more information.

Our *Welfare Benefits and Tax Credits Handbook*, published anually, includes detailed information on personal independence payment. It also tells you all you need to know about entitlement to benefits and tax credits.

Getting advice

Your local citizens advice bureau or other advice centre can give you advice and support on benefits. See www.citizensadvice.org.uk if you live in England or Wales, or www.cas.org.uk if you live in Scotland.

CPAG has an advice line for advisers and support workers.

For advisers in England and Wales:

Telephone: 020 7812 5231, Monday to Friday 10am to 12pm and 2pm to 4pm

For advisers in Scotland:
Telephone: 0141 552 0552, Monday to Thursday 10am to 4pm and Friday 10am to 12pm.
Email: advice@cpagscotland.org.uk

Contents

Chapter 1
Introduction

This chapter covers:

1. What is personal independence payment?

2. Personal independence payment and disability living allowance

3. What does this guide cover?

What you need to know

- Personal independence payment is a benefit for people aged 16 to 64 that you may qualify for if a health condition or disability affects your ability to carry out a range of everyday activities.

- It has two 'components' – a daily living component and a mobility component. You can qualify for one or both. Each component is paid at one of two rates.

- You normally claim personal independence payment by telephone and must then complete a questionnaire and attend a consultation with a 'healthcare professional'.

- You are assessed on how your health condition or disability affects your ability to carry out 12 everyday activities.

- You are normally awarded personal independence payment for a fixed period and then reassessed.

- If you are refused personal independence payment, you can ask for a 'mandatory reconsideration' and then appeal.

- Personal independence payment is gradually replacing disability living allowance for people of working age.

1. What is personal independence payment?

Personal independence payment is a benefit for people of working age (normally aged 16 to 64 inclusive) with an illness or disability that affects their ability to carry out a range of everyday activities for at least a year.

It was introduced for new claimants in Great Britain in 2013. It was introduced in June 2016 in Northern Ireland. This book explains the rules in Great Britain. Although most of the rules in Northern Ireland are similar, some important things are different.

People aged 16 or over who were under 65 on 8 April 2013 and who currently get disability living allowance will be transferred to personal independence payment over the next few years.

Personal independence payment is administered and paid by the Department for Work and Pensions. It is not 'means tested' (it can be paid regardless of how much income or capital you have) and it is not taxable. You do not have to have made any national insurance contributions to qualify and you can get it whether you are in or out of work. It is paid on top of most other benefits.

Personal independence payment is made up of two 'components' – a daily living component, paid if you have difficulty carrying out specified daily living activities, and a mobility component, paid if you have difficulty carrying out specified mobility activities. You may qualify for one or both components. Each component is paid at a standard and an enhanced (higher) rate.

Entitlement to the different components and rates of personal independence payment can also qualify you and your carer for other benefits and schemes, including carer's allowance, a blue badge for parking, exemption from road tax and help from the Motability scheme.

Although personal independence payment is designed to help with the extra costs of ill health or disability, you can use the money in any way you wish and do not have to account for how you spend it.

How are you assessed and paid?

You must normally make a claim for personal independence payment by telephone. You must then usually fill in a questionnaire about how your health or disability affects you, and attend a consultation with a 'healthcare professional' who assesses your difficulties and may give you a short medical examination. The healthcare professional sends a report to the Department for Work and Pensions (DWP), where a 'case manager' decides whether you qualify for personal independence payment.

To qualify, you must show that your ability to carry out a range of everyday activities is limited because of your physical or mental condition. There are 10 daily living activities and two mobility activities. Each activity is described by a number of statements (called 'descriptors') which reflect different levels of ability. Each descriptor is given a score; the greater the level of difficulty described, the higher the score. You can only score points for one descriptor within each activity. The DWP decides which descriptors you satisfy. You must score at least eight points to qualify for the standard rate of the daily living or mobility component. If you score 12 points or more, you qualify for the enhanced rate.

Awards of personal independence payment are usually made for a fixed period. You are paid by credit transfer into your bank account, usually every four weeks. You can be reassessed at any time, although this normally happens when your award is coming to an end, when you report a change in your condition, or if the DWP thinks your case should be reviewed.

If you are refused personal independence payment, or receive less money than you think you should get, you can ask the DWP to do a 'mandatory reconsideration' and then appeal to an independent tribunal.

Special rules apply if you have a terminal illness, or if you are in a care home, hospital or in prison.

2. Personal independence payment and disability living allowance

Personal independence payment is gradually replacing disability living allowance for people of working age (aged 16 to 64). You can still get disability living allowance for children under 16 and attendance allowance if you are 65 or over.

If you are not already getting disability living allowance, you cannot make a claim for it if you are aged 16 or over. You must claim personal independence payment instead. If you are currently getting disability living allowance and turn 16, you are normally required to claim personal independence payment instead at that point. If you were under 65 on 8 April 2013 and still get disability living allowance, you will be asked to claim personal independence payment over the next few years. See Chapter 10 for more details.

Box A
Personal independence payment and disability living allowance: how are they the same?

- Both are cash benefits to help pay for the extra costs that result from having a long-term health condition or disability.

- Both are 'non-means-tested' and non-taxable benefits. They can be paid on top of most other benefits and give eligibility to other benefits, such as carer's allowance, and the blue badge and Motability schemes.

- Both have similar special rules for people who have a terminal illness, or who are in a care home.

- Both have two 'components' and the amounts paid are mostly the same.

Box B
Personal independence payment and disability living allowance: how are they different?

- Personal independence payment has only two rates of the daily living component. There is no equivalent amount to the disability living allowance low rate care component.

- To get personal independence payment your needs must normally be expected to last for at least one year (instead of nine months to get disability living allowance).

- The disability conditions for personal independence payment are more restrictive than for disability living allowance. There is less provision for help needed to carry out the full range of everyday activities (including social activities).

- The assessment procedure for personal independence payment is more rigorous. There are face-to-face consultations, and more regular reviews and reassessments of awards, the majority of which are for a fixed period.

Why was disability living allowance replaced?

The government's case for replacing disability living allowance with personal independence payment was that disability living allowance had become an outdated benefit. Disability living allowance was criticised for having complex and subjective assessment criteria, and inconsistent decision making, resulting in too many awards and too few reviews of awards.

The government says that personal independence payment is a more 'active and enabling benefit'. It is intended to assess people more objectively, accurately and frequently, resulting in more consistent decision making. By focusing entitlement on those most in need of additional support, the government hopes to eventually save around 20 per cent of the cost of disability living allowance (compared with the expected expenditure on people aged 16 and over if it had not been replaced).

3. What does this guide cover?

This guide covers the main aspects of personal independence payment, including:

- who can claim and the main conditions you must meet to be entitled (Chapter 2)
- how to claim and how you are assessed (Chapter 3)
- details of the disability assessment criteria, including the activities you are tested against and the points you must score to qualify for an award (Chapters 4, 5 and 6)
- how you can challenge decisions or qualify for a higher award if how your condition affects you changes (Chapter 7)
- how personal independence payment is affected if you have a terminal illness or are in hospital, a care home or in prison (Chapter 8)
- how personal independence payment can help you qualify for other benefits (Chapter 9)
- what happens if you currently get disability living allowance (Chapter 10)

This guide does not cover the possible changes to personal independence payment that may be made in Scotland in the future. It is not currently known when this will happen and what will change.

Chapter 2
Who can get personal independence payment

This chapter covers:

1. Who can get personal independence payment?

2. What are the rules about your age?

3. What are the nationality and residence rules?

What you need to know

- You must have a disability or long-term health condition to get personal independence payment.

- To get personal independence payment, you must be 16 or over.

- Normally, you cannot claim personal independence payment for the first time if you are 65 or over.

- There are complicated rules preventing you from getting personal independence payment in some circumstances if you have recently spent time abroad or if you are not a British citizen.

1. Who can get personal independence payment?

You might be able to get personal independence payment if you have a long-term health condition or a disability.

If you meet the basic rules of entitlement, you can choose to claim personal independence payment even if you currently get disability living allowance. It is important to think carefully about this, as your disability living allowance will end once you claim personal independence payment. You cannot change your mind and make another claim for disability living allowance in the future. Use the information in Chapter 10 to help you decide.

What the law says

The basic rules of entitlement

- To get personal independence payment, you must meet conditions relating to:
  - your age
  - your nationality
  - your country of residence
  - the effect your health condition or disability has on you.

- Personal independence payment has a mobility component and a daily living component, each paid at a standard or enhanced rate depending on the difficulties you have with a set list of activities. To qualify for a component, your needs must normally be expected to last for a year or more (unless you are terminally ill).

Part 4 Welfare Reform Act 2012

Chapters 4, 5 and 6 cover the rules on how the effects of your health condition or disability are assessed to see if you qualify for personal independence payment.

Even if you qualify, personal independence payment might not be paid to you if you are in prison, in hospital, or in a care home. The rules about this are explained in Chapter 8.

You can qualify for personal independence payment regardless of your income and savings, and whether or not you are working. You do not have to pay national insurance contributions to qualify.

2. What are the rules about your age?

You can claim personal independence payment if you are between the ages of 16 and 64. In some cases, you can get personal independence payment after you have reached 65.

Are you at least 16?

You cannot get personal independence payment until you are 16. If you are younger than 16, your parent or another adult can claim disability living allowance on your behalf.

If you do not get disability living allowance and you are 16 or over, you should claim personal independence payment as soon as you can. This is because your entitlement cannot start before the day you make your claim. Chapter 3 explains how to claim.

If you are already getting disability living allowance and you turn 16, the Department for Work and Pensions (DWP) will write to you telling you that you must claim personal independence payment instead. Your disability living allowance ends when your personal independence payment claim is decided. The only exceptions to this are if you have a terminal illness or are in hospital when you turn 16. However, if you leave hospital or your disability living allowance award is due to run out, you can still be asked to claim personal independence payment at that point.

See Chapter 10 for more information on transferring to personal independence payment.

EXAMPLE

16-year-olds

Andy turns 16 in December 2016. He gets disability living allowance. Just after he turns 16, he receives a letter from the DWP telling him that he needs to claim personal independence payment. He does so and his disability living allowance ends shortly after the decision is made about his entitlement to personal independence payment.

Are you 65 or over?

Normally, you must make a claim for personal independence payment before you turn 65. If your health condition or disability starts to affect you after you turn 65, you are not entitled to personal independence payment and must claim attendance allowance instead. If you already get attendance allowance, you cannot get personal independence payment.

If you claim personal independence payment just before you turn 65 and you meet the entitlement conditions, an award can be made to you, even if the decision on your claim is not made until after your 65th birthday.

If you already get personal independence payment when you turn 65, your award normally has a set date on which it ends. You can renew your award by making a new claim in the months before it ends, but you must be claiming for the same disability or health condition, or a new condition that has developed from it. You can also claim personal independence payment again if it is less than a year since your award ended, even though you are over 65. Again, your claim must be based on the same condition or a new one that has developed from it. There are special rules about when you can get the mobility component once you have turned 65.

If you get, or you used to get, disability living allowance, personal independence payment or attendance allowance and are now 65, the rules on which benefit you can get are complicated and depend on when you turned 65 and which benefit you received most recently (see the table opposite). Like personal independence payment, attendance allowance and disability living allowance are often awarded to you for a fixed period, at the end of which you need to make a new claim.

If you were under 65 on 8 April 2013, you are now 65 or over, and you stopped getting disability living allowance less than a year ago, you can claim personal independence payment no matter what your health condition is, provided you meet the normal rules of entitlement. The special rules about the mobility component described in the next section do not apply to you the first time you claim personal independence payment.

If you are getting personal independence payment and you are now 65 or over, you can ask for your award to be looked at again because your circumstances have changed. You can be awarded a different rate of the daily living component and, if you were getting the mobility component, you can qualify for the daily living component for the first time even if you are 65 or over. However, there are special rules that limit your entitlement to the mobility component once you are 65.

Which benefit can you claim?

When were you 65?	Which benefit do you currently get or did you most recently get?	Which benefit can you claim?
Any time	You have not received any disability living allowance or personal independence payment for over a year, or you get or used to get attendance allowance	Attendance allowance
On or before 8 April 2013	Disability living allowance, or it stopped less than a year ago	Disability living allowance
After 8 April 2013	Disability living allowance or personal independence payment, which you still get	Personal independence payment
After 8 April 2013	Personal independence payment or disability living allowance which ended less than a year ago	You can choose to claim either personal independence payment or attendance allowance (get specialist advice about which benefit to claim)

How is your mobility component affected when you are 65?

You cannot qualify for the mobility component of personal independence payment for the first time if your mobility is first affected by your condition after you turn 65.

> **EXAMPLE**
>
> **65-year-olds**
>
> Clarice has multiple sclerosis. She was first awarded personal independence payment in January 2016. She then goes into remission and her award ends on 24 October 2016 after she reports the change in her circumstances. She turned 65 on 31 January 2016.
>
> By March 2017, Clarice's condition has worsened again. Although she is 65, she can make a new claim for personal independence payment as it is less than a year since her previous award ended. Clarice could also choose to claim attendance allowance, but she gets advice at her local citizen's advice bureau and is told that it is better for her to claim personal independence payment again.

If you are 65, and already get the mobility component, you can continue to receive it until your award ends. You can then make a renewal claim and continue to receive the same rate of the mobility component. Your mobility needs must arise from the same condition as your previous award or from a new condition that has developed from it.

If your needs have decreased, you may be awarded the standard rate rather than your previous enhanced rate. However, you cannot have the rate you are paid increased from the standard rate to the enhanced rate, even if your mobility needs have increased.

If the Department for Work and Pensions changes your personal independence payment award after you turn 65 (for example, because your circumstances have changed or your original award was not correct), you are only awarded the mobility component if you currently get it, or you used to get it less than a year ago but it stopped. You can only be awarded the same rate of mobility component again if your mobility needs arise from the same condition as your previous award. You cannot have your award increased from the standard rate to the enhanced rate. You can be awarded the standard rate if you used to get the enhanced rate.

EXAMPLE

Mobility component for 65-year-olds

Dolores is 66. She has arthritis and gets the standard rate of personal independence payment daily living component and the standard rate of the mobility component. She is involved in a road traffic accident and is left paralysed from the waist down. She asks for her award to be looked at again. Her daily living component award is changed to the enhanced rate, but she cannot be awarded the enhanced rate of the mobility component. She meets the normal entitlement conditions, but her mobility component award cannot be increased because the accident happened after she turned 65.

3. What are the nationality and residence rules?

The rules can prevent you from getting personal independence payment if you are not a UK national or if you have recently spent time abroad. This is a complicated area of law, and you are likely to need specialist advice.

Are you a foreign national?

If you are a national of a country outside the European Economic Area, you are likely to be classified as a 'person subject to immigration control'. Most people who are subject to immigration control cannot claim personal independence payment. If you are in any doubt about whether you are a person subject to immigration control, it is vital that you get specialist immigration advice before you make a claim for personal independence payment. This is because making a claim when you are not allowed to do so can affect your right to stay in the UK.

If you are a national of a European Economic Area country, you can claim personal independence payment. However, the rules for people who have spent time abroad may mean you do not qualify.

There are complicated rules that may mean you can claim personal independence payment if you are a family member of a European national or if you have been helped to come to the UK by a friend or relative who is your 'sponsor'. Get specialist advice if this may apply to you, before you make a claim.

Have you spent time abroad?

The rules on residence apply to everyone who claims personal independence payment, even if you are a UK national.

What the law says

Residence in Great Britain

To get personal independence payment you must normally:
- be present in Great Britain now
- have been present in Great Britain for two of the last three years
- be 'habitually resident' in the UK or Ireland (including the Isle of Man and the Channel Islands)

Regulation 16 Social Security (Personal Independence Payment) Regulations 2013

There are a number of exceptions to the standard rules on residence.

- If you are 'terminally ill', you do not have to have been in Great Britain for two of the last three years.

- If you work in certain occupations, such as aircraft cabin crew, sailors or oil rig workers, time spent outside Great Britain for work can be ignored. You must be a UK employee for this rule to apply.

- If you or a member of your family you live with are serving abroad in the UK armed forces, the rules treat you as if you are in Great Britain.

- You are treated as if you are still in Great Britain during certain 'temporary absences'.

- If you have spent time elsewhere in Europe, special European rules can help you to meet the standard tests using time spent living in another European country. You should get expert advice.

Box A

What does 'habitually resident' mean?

The meaning of 'habitual residence' has been defined by many court decisions over the years.

- You must intend to live in Great Britain for some time in the future (although not necessarily forever). Things like giving up your former home in another country, whether you still keep your money abroad, where your close family live and what they are doing, and registering with a doctor in the UK may be relevant.

- Normally, you must have been living here for an 'appreciable period' of time to become habitually resident. This is often, but not always, between one and three months. However, if you previously lived here and have returned after spending time abroad, you may be habitually resident as soon as you return, depending on your circumstances.

- If you go abroad for a holiday, you do not stop being habitually resident in the UK.

- If you are serving abroad in the UK armed forces or you live with a family member who is, you are still treated as habitually resident in the UK.

European rules mean you may be able to get the the daily living component of personal independence payment if you are habitually resident elsewhere in Europe but still have a strong link to the UK benefits system.

If your claim for personal independence payment is refused because the Department for Work and Pensions (DWP) decides you are not habitually resident, you should get specialist advice to help you challenge the decision.

EXAMPLE

The residence rules

Debs is a UK national who has been living and working in the USA for the last five years. When she is diagnosed with cancer, she gives up her job and her apartment and returns to live permanently with her family in London. She claims personal independence payment, but her claim is refused on the grounds that she has not been in the UK for two of the last three years.

Two months later, her consultant tells her that the cancer has spread and that she probably only has a few months to live. She makes a new claim for personal independence payment and asks her consultant to confirm her prognosis on Form DS1500.

Debs is awarded personal independence payment, as it is accepted that she is habitually resident. Because she has a terminal illness the length of time she has been in Great Britain during the past three years does not matter.

You can continue to get personal independence payment during part of a 'temporary absence' from Great Britain, as the rules treat you as if you are still in Great Britain. The definition of 'temporary absence' is that your absence must not be expected to last longer than a year. Your personal independence payment continues for the first 13 weeks you are abroad, or for the first 26 weeks if you go abroad specifically for the purpose of getting medical treatment. If you are abroad in another European country, special European rules mean that you might be able to get the daily living component of personal independence payment for longer. You should get specialist advice about this, and always inform the DWP if you are going abroad.

What CPAG says

If you are affected by the residence rules

This is a very complicated and fast-changing area of the law. We suggest that if you are refused personal independence payment due to these rules, you try to get specialist advice to help you to work out if you may be able to successfully challenge the decision. You may also need to check what benefits you may qualify for from another European country.

Further information

The residence and presence tests for personal independence payment are explained in more detail in Part 11 of CPAG's *Welfare Benefits and Tax Credits Handbook* and CPAG's *Benefits for Migrants Handbook.*
On www.gov.uk there is *Advice for Decision Making,* produced by the Department for Work and Pensions for its own staff. Chapter P1 sets out the basic entitlement conditions for personal independence payment, and chapter C2 looks at 'international issues'.

Chapter 3
Claims, assessments and getting paid

This chapter covers:

1. How do you make a claim?

2. When should you claim?

3. How are you assessed?

4. Getting paid

What you need to know

- You normally claim personal independence payment by telephone. If you cannot do so, you can use a claim form.

- You should claim as soon as think you might qualify to avoid losing money. You can sometimes make an advance claim.

- After you claim, you must usually complete a questionnaire about how your health condition or disability affects you. Most people must also attend a face-to-face consultation with a 'healthcare professional'.

- Personal independence payment is usually awarded for a fixed period.

- You are likely to be reassessed about one year before your award is due to end.

- If you are refused personal independence payment, you can ask for a 'mandatory reconsideration' and then appeal.

1. How do you make a claim?

How do you start your claim?

You must normally claim personal independence payment by telephone on 0800 917 2222 (textphone 0800 917 7777). The lines are open between 8am and 6pm, Monday to Friday. The calls are free from most landlines and mobiles, but some providers may charge. If you are worried about the cost of the call, ask the Department for Work and Pensions (DWP) to ring you back.

If you find it hard to use a phone, someone else can ring for you and give the required information, provided you are present during the call and can confirm that the other person is acting with your permission.

If you have difficulty speaking and understanding English, the DWP can arrange for an interpreter to speak to you in your own language during the call.

If you use British Sign Language to communicate, you can make a claim by video call. Go to www.gov.uk/pip/how-to-claim for details.

If you are unable to manage your own affairs and have someone who acts for you (such as an 'appointee' or a person with a 'power of attorney'), s/he should make the claim on your behalf. If no one has been appointed to act for you, someone can apply to the DWP to be your appointee.

If you have a terminal illness, someone else can also make a claim on your behalf.

If you are unable to make your claim by telephone and have no one to support you, you can use a claim form.

The government plans to introduce online claims for personal independence payment in the future. If this would be easier for you, check www.gov.uk to see if this service is available.

What are you asked during the call?

Box A
Information for your claim
Have the following information ready for your telephone claim:

- full name and date of birth
- national insurance number (if you do not have a number, you must apply for one. You should telephone the number to make a claim and ask about this. You are then sent a personal independence payment claim form)
- full address, including postcode and contact phone numbers
- details of any communication requirements that you have – for example, if you need letters sent to you in Braille or large print, or recorded on to an audio CD
- nationality and any immigration restrictions
- usual country of residence and details of any time spent abroad, if this was for more than four weeks at a time in the last three years
- details of any work in, national insurance contributions paid in, and pensions or benefits received from, another 'European Economic Area' country or Switzerland
- dates of current or recent stays in a hospital, hospice or care home
- name, address and phone number of your GP or other healthcare professional who supports you (you are asked to give your consent for the Department for Work and Pensions (DWP) to contact her/him to obtain further information about your health condition or disability)
- details of whether you have a condition that affects your mental health, learning, development, behaviour or causes memory problems (in case you require more help or consideration during the assessment process)
- bank or building society account details for payment of your personal independence payment

During the call, you are asked for information about yourself to establish your identity and that you meet the basic conditions of entitlement for personal independence payment. If you cannot establish your identity over the telephone, your claim should still be taken, but you may need to provide further information and evidence before it is accepted that you are who you say you are.

At this stage, you are not asked to give details about your health or disability and how it affects you. The call is likely to take about 15 minutes.

If you do not have all the information listed in Box A when you call, you can ring back to provide it. Some of the information is required for your claim to be completed. You must provide any required missing information within one month (or a longer period allowed by the DWP) for the claim to be valid and start from the date of your original call. Once all the information is complete, you must declare that it is all correct, as far as you know and believe. The claim is then processed by the DWP.

Who can complete a claim form?

If you are unable to make your claim by phone, you can request a claim form (form PIP1). Telephone 0800 917 2222 (textphone 0800 917 7777). Someone can phone on your behalf if you are present and give your consent to the Department for Work and Pensions (DWP). If you cannot use the phone and have no one to help you, you can request a claim form by writing to: Personal Independence Payment New Claims, Post Handling Site B, Wolverhampton WV99 1AH. However, this will delay the date of your claim so it is better to phone and ask for a form if you are able to do this.

You can also ask for a home visit by a DWP visiting officer to help you complete the form, if you cannot do this yourself and have no one to help you.

The claim form is personalised for your use only and should not be used by anyone else. You can ask for a large print or Braille version if you have a visual impairment.

The claim form asks for the same information as a telephone claim and should be returned by post in the envelope provided.

You have one month to complete and return the form for your claim to start on the day of your initial call. If you need longer than this, you should explain why and the time can be extended if it is reasonable to do so.

Are you terminally ill?

If you are 'terminally ill', someone else can make a claim for personal independence payment on your behalf, either by telephone or by using a claim form. This can be with or without your knowledge.

You are treated as terminally ill if you have a progressive disease and you can be reasonably expected to die within six months. You, or the person claiming for you, should get Form DS1500, confirming this, from your consultant, GP, nurse or social worker and send it to the Department for Work and Pensions (DWP) with your claim (unless one has already been sent within the past six months).

The DWP informs you that a claim has been made, but does not refer to your having a terminal illness. If you are claiming on behalf of someone else, you should therefore tell her/him that a claim for personal independence payment has been made.

2. When should you claim?

In order to avoid losing money, you should make a claim as soon as you think you may qualify for personal independence payment. This is because you can only be paid from the date of your claim. The only exception to this is if you currently get disability living allowance. See Chapter 10 for things to think about when deciding whether to claim personal independence payment if you currently get disablity living allowance.

The date of your claim is normally the date you telephone to make a claim (or request a claim form by phone), so long as you provide all the required information within one month (or longer if the Department for Work and Pensions (DWP) allows this). Your award of personal independence payment can only start from the day your claim is finalised in this way.

You cannot normally qualify for personal independence payment until you have met the conditions for the daily living or mobility component for at least three months. However, you can claim personal independence payment in advance if the DWP thinks you are likely to qualify within three months. You are paid from the date you qualify.

EXAMPLE

The three-month requirement

Deborah has a stroke on 30 July 2016 and is admitted to hospital. She is discharged on 30 August and claims personal independence payment later that day. She is assessed as meeting the conditions for an award from 30 July. She is awarded personal independence payment from 30 October, which is when she has completed the three-month qualifying period.

3. How are you assessed?

To qualify for personal independence payment, you must show that your ability to carry out a range of everyday activities is limited because of your health condition or disability. Chapters 4, 5 and 6 cover this in more detail.

If your claim shows that you satisfy the basic conditions of entitlement for personal independence payment, you are normally sent a questionnaire (form PIP2) to complete about how your health condition or disability affects you, together with an explanatory booklet. The questionnaire is personalised for your use only and should not be used by anyone else.

If you have claimed on the basis of having a terminal illness, you do not need to complete a questionnaire and your claim is passed to a 'healthcare professional' for an assessment. If you explained that you had a mental health, learning, developmental, behavioural or memory condition when you made your claim, the Department for Work and Pensions (DWP) can also send your claim to be assessed without you having to complete a questionnaire. This is discretionary, so if you are sent a questionnaire you should complete it even if you have one of these conditions.

What the law says

The time limit

- If you are required to complete and submit a questionnaire and you fail, 'without good reason', to do so within one month, or such longer period as the DWP considers reasonable, you will be issued a decision stating you are not entitled to personal independence payment.

- 'Good reason' can include anything which explains why you were unable to send in the questionnaire on time, such as if you were too unwell, the nature of your disability, or you were abroad or dealing with a domestic emergency.

Regulations 8 and 10 Social Security (Personal Independence Payment) Regulations 2013

You must sign the declaration on the questionnaire and return it in the envelope provided within a calendar month. If you have not returned it after 20 days, you should receive a reminder letter. If you need more time, ring the personal independence payment helpline on 0345 850 3322 (textphone 0345 601 6677) and explain your situation. You can be given more time if it is reasonable to do so.

If you receive a decision stating you are not entitled to personal independence payment because you failed to return the questionnaire, you can request a 'mandatory reconsideration' and then appeal. See Chapter 7 for more details on how to do this. Explain why you did not return it and send any evidence that you have confirming this, such as a letter from your GP if you were ill, or details of any postal problems you are having if the questionnaire went missing. You should also make a new claim, in case the decision is not changed.

Box B
The questionnaire

The questionnaire asks for details of:

- professionals you see who can provide information about your condition – for example, your GP, or a doctor, nurse, occupational therapist, physiotherapist, social worker, counsellor or support worker (if there is not room for all of the people who help you, add their details in the 'Additional Information' section at the end of the questionnaire)
- your health condition or disability, and any medication you take and treatment you have
- the difficulty you have carrying out the everyday activities on which you are assessed. These are:
  - preparing food and cooking
  - eating and drinking
  - managing your treatments
  - washing and bathing
  - managing your toilet needs
  - dressing and undressing
  - speaking and hearing
  - reading
  - mixing with other people
  - making decisions about money
  - going out
  - moving around
- details of any special arrangements that you would need for a face-to-face consultation

How should you complete the questionnaire?

It is important to complete the questionnaire as fully as possible and give all the relevant information about your difficulties.

- Read Chapters 4, 5 and 6 of this book so you understand the assessment criteria. In particular, remember that it is not your condition itself that qualifies you for personal independence payment, but how this affects your ability to carry out a specified range of activities. Identify the statements (known as 'descriptors') under each activity you think you satisfy. This will help you to decide what information it is relevant to give.

- If you do not have a firm diagnosis, give a general description of how you are affected by your condition and make sure you explain on the questionnaire what steps are being taken to work out what is causing your symptoms.

- There are tick boxes for whether you use any aids or appliances, and whether you need help from another person. Explain the difficulties you have and the help you need in the boxes provided. You can include additional information at the end of the form, including details of carers and relatives who know or help you. You can also send additional supporting evidence with the questionnaire.

- You may need to explain whether you can carry out an activity safely, to an acceptable standard, repeatedly and within a reasonable time period. If your condition fluctuates, it is important to give information about your good and bad days, how your needs vary during the day, and the proportion of days on which you can and cannot manage the relevant activities. You may find it helpful to keep a diary, recording how your condition affects you on a daily basis. You can use this to help you complete the questionnaire, or you can send a copy of it with the questionnaire.

- Read the guidance in the questionnaire and information booklet. This includes useful information and examples of the type of help you may need.

- Complete the form clearly and legibly in ink. It will be scanned and sent electronically to a 'healthcare professional' and must be readable. Make sure you read and sign the declaration at the end, confirming that, as far as you are aware, the information you have given is correct.

- If possible, keep a copy, so you can read it before you attend your consultation.

Do you need help completing the questionnaire?

If you need help completing your questionnaire, consult a local advice centre, such as a citizens advice bureau. You may also be able to get advice online or by telephone from a disability organisation specialising in your condition. A friend, relative or carer could help you complete the questionnaire, provided you sign the declaration.

The personal independence payment helpline (0345 850 3322; textphone 0345 601 6677) can help with any general or basic enquiries you have and may also be able to tell you about local advice services offering more specialist help. Someone from the Department for Work and Pensions (DWP) may be able to phone you back to give you further advice and help.

If you are unable to complete the questionnaire yourself and cannot get help, the DWP can arrange for you to be visited at home.

What CPAG says

Help with the questionnaire

It is likely that you will underestimate the difficulties that you have with the activities in the questionnaire, often as your way of managing becomes 'normal' for you if there is no help available. CPAG suggests that you try to get help from a local advice centre to complete the questionnaire. If you are unsure of your ability to explain the help that you need fully, you could take someone who knows you well to help you to explain your needs fully to the advice worker. If waiting for an appointment means that it is going to take you more than one month to return the questionnaire, remember to contact the helpline and ask for an extension of time.

What evidence should you include?

Your claim may be helped if you send copies of any written evidence you have that supports it. This could include letters and reports from your GP, other health professionals, a social worker, carer or support worker. If you have kept a diary with details of how your condition affects you on a daily basis, you could also send a copy. You should only send evidence that is relevant and up to date, and which supports and confirms the information you have given in the questionnaire. If you are not sure whether evidence is helpful, check how closely it relates to the activities in the personal independence payment assessment – these are explained in Chapters 5 and 6.

Only send photocopies (not the originals) of the documents you have. List the documents you are sending in the box on page 2 of the questionnaire, and send them with the questionnaire in the envelope provided. Do not delay sending your questionnaire while you are waiting for further evidence; you can send the evidence separately when you get it.

Who assesses you?

The assessment of whether you satisfy the disability or health conditions for personal independence payment is carried out in two stages.

- First, you are assessed by a 'healthcare professional'. In most cases, you must attend a face-to-face consultation with her/him. S/he sends a report to the Department for Work and Pensions (DWP), setting out details of the assessment and giving her/his opinion of which 'descriptors' apply to you and when you should be reassessed.

- Your case is then looked at by a DWP 'case manager'. S/he decides whether you are entitled to personal independence payment based on all the evidence, including the healthcare professional's report and the questionnaire. S/he can seek further evidence or clarification from the healthcare professional or other sources if necessary before making the final decision. Note that the DWP decides whether you are entitled to personal independence payment. The healthcare professional only provides advice to the DWP case manager.

Two private companies carry out personal independence payment medical assessments on behalf of the DWP:

- Atos Healthcare, covering London, southern England, northern England and Scotland
- Capita Business Services, covering central England, Wales and Northern Ireland

There are some differences in the way the two companies provide the service. You can find more information on their websites: www.atoshealthcare.com/pip and www.capita-pip.co.uk. Both must operate in accordance with their contracts and service-level agreements with the DWP, and must take into account the detailed guidance on assessments issued by the DWP. The assessments are carried out by trained healthcare professionals on behalf of the two companies. A 'healthcare professional' could be a:

- registered doctor
- level 1 nurse
- paramedic
- physiotherapist
- occupational therapist

What happens at the initial assessment?

The Department for Work and Pensions (DWP) sends a copy of your questionnaire and any other relevant evidence to Atos or Capita. The healthcare professional then decides whether further evidence is needed and whether or not a consultation is required.

If the health professional thinks that additional evidence would be helpful, s/he can request a report from your GP, hospital doctor or other health professional listed on your claim form or questionnaire. Further evidence can be sought from your social worker, support worker or other professional referred to in your case papers. You may also be telephoned for further information about how your condition affects you.

If you have obtained additional evidence that may be helpful to your claim since completing the questionnaire, send a copy of it to the DWP with a letter asking them to forward it to Atos or Capita for consideration.

Who does not need to attend a consultation?

Most people must attend a consultation with a 'healthcare professional'. However, in some circumstances, s/he can complete an assessment and send a report to the Department for Work and Pensions (DWP) based on the evidence in the papers, without seeing you. This should always happen if your claim is on the basis of a terminal illness and you have confirmed this with appropriate evidence. If you are terminally ill, your assessment should be completed and returned to the DWP within 48 hours.

You may not need to attend a consultation if there is sufficient evidence in your papers for the healthcare professional to provide advice to the DWP, or if there is strong evidence that you will find a face-to-face consultation stressful or distressing.

Attending a consultation

Both Atos and Capita use 'healthcare professionals' based at dedicated assessment centres, or in local NHS or private health centres or clinics. You are usually required to attend at the place where the healthcare professional is based. This should be accessible for disabled people, and by public transport within a maximum of 90 minutes' travelling time. If you are unable, or would find it difficult, to travel because of your condition, you can request a consultation at home. Explain why you need this and support your request with medical or other evidence. If a home consultation is refused, you can complain, using the Atos or Capita complaints procedure.

You should receive a letter with details of your appointment and what to take with you (including proof of identity and any new evidence you have about your health condition or disability). You must be given at least seven days' written notice of your appointment (unless you agree to accept shorter notice).

If you cannot attend, phone the number on your appointment letter and ask for another appointment. You can also phone if you have any special requirements, including if you need an interpreter, or if you want a consultation with a person of the same gender.

The cost of your travel expenses can be reimbursed. If you take someone with you, her/his travel expenses can also be reimbursed. You should be sent a claim form with your appointment letter, but you cannot claim in advance. You are paid by cheque or directly into your bank account. You can claim for the cost of public transport or travel by car (including any parking charges). If you need to travel by taxi because you cannot use public transport or it is not available, phone the number on your appointment letter in advance about this.

What happens at the consultation?

The consultation is with a trained 'healthcare professional'. You can take someone, such as a friend, relative, carer or support worker, with you if this would be helpful. As well as giving you support, s/he can take part in the discussion and help explain how your condition or disability affects you. If you want to take more than one person with you, you should ask about this in advance by calling the number on your appointment letter.

The aim of the consultation is to enable the healthcare professional to gather evidence about how your health or disability affects you, so s/he can advise the Department for Work and Pensions (DWP) which 'descriptors' apply to you.

S/he should speak to you politely and clearly, asking you open questions and giving you the time and opportunity to explain properly the impact of your health condition or disability.

Although s/he will probably need to record information on a computer system during the consultation, this should not be done at the expense of listening to you or maintaining regular eye contact while you are speaking.

There is no audio recording of your consultation. If you want to record the consultation yourself, you should arrange this in advance by calling the number on your appointment letter. You will need to record the consultation on your own equipment and give a copy to the healthcare professional at the end. You cannot make video recordings, computers cannot be used to make recordings, and your recording equipment must be able to produce two copies of a CD or audio tape immediately at the end of the consultation.

There is no set length of time for the consultation, but it may typically take about an hour.

What questions are you asked?

- You are asked about your condition, including what it is, when it began, what symptoms you experience and whether they are constant or variable, and what treatment you have had or are having, including any medication you take.

- You are also asked about your work history and social life, such as where you live, whether your home has disability adaptations, whether anyone lives with you and supports you, and the leisure and social activities you do or can no longer do.

- You are then asked questions about how your illness or disability affects your everyday life. This is usually done by asking you to talk through a 'typical day', explaining what you do and what difficulties you have carrying out everyday tasks, including getting up, washing and dressing, preparing food and eating, managing your treatment and medication, managing your toilet needs, communicating with others, getting out and about, shopping and any hobbies or pastimes.

Will you be examined?

If appropriate, the healthcare professional may carry out a short medical examination relevant to your condition. You must give your consent to this and may be asked to recline on an examination couch. You should never be required to remove your underwear or to undergo a breast, rectal or genital examination.

What 'observations' are made?

Throughout the consultation, the healthcare professional makes her/his own observations about your physical and psychological abilities and limitations, including on how you stand, sit, move around, answer questions and behave.

Box C
Preparing for the consultation

- Read your questionnaire and any other evidence you have submitted before you attend. This will help ensure that the information you give during the consultation is consistent.

- Read Chapters 4, 5 and 6 of this book, so you are familiar with the 'descriptors' you satisfy. When you answer questions about a typical day and how your condition affects you, focus on showing that you satisfy the descriptors.

- Provide information about any aids and appliances you use, the help you need from other people, and whether you can carry out an activity reliably. If your condition fluctuates, give information about your good and bad days, and the proportion of days on which you can and cannot undertake relevant activities. Make sure you explain difficulties with managing the activities at certain times of the day.

- Focus on the difficulties you face. Even if you manage to carry out certain tasks, explain if, and how, this is difficult for you. Remember that the test is not whether you get help, but whether you need help.

- Prepare what you want to say about your condition, your symptoms, your 'typical day', and the difficulties you face with everyday tasks. Bear in mind that the healthcare professional is unlikely to be a specialist in your condition, so you may need to explain its nature and the symptoms.

- Take someone with you if you want support. S/he may also be able to give useful information about your difficulties. Talk through the above points with her/him beforehand, so you are both clear about what you want to say.

- Allow plenty of time for the journey, so you arrive in time and are as relaxed as possible. Take details of your medication and any new evidence that is relevant to your claim. If you have had to take extra medication to manage to get to the consultation, explain this.

Are you unhappy with the consultation?

If you are unhappy with the way you were treated during the consultation, you can make a complaint. You may be unhappy about how you were spoken to, listened to or examined, or about the venue or waiting times. You should be given information about the complaints procedure at the end of your consultation.

Written complaints must be acknowledged within two working days, and you should normally receive a full response within 20 working days.

Making a complaint should not affect your claim for personal independence payment.

What happens if you do not attend the consultation?

If you do not attend or participate in a consultation and do not have a good reason, your claim can be rejected. You receive a decision stating that you are not entitled to personal independence payment. If you cannot attend an appointment, you should ring Atos or Capita on the number provided as soon as possible to explain why.

What the law says

Failing to attend the consultation

- You must have received at least seven days' written notice of your appointment (unless you agreed to shorter notice).

- 'Good reason' can include anything which explains why you were unable to attend the consultation, such as if you were too ill or disabled, you were abroad or you were dealing with a domestic emergency.

Regulations 9 and 10 Social Security (Personal Independence Payment) Regulations 2013

If you receive a decision stating you are not entitled to personal independence payment because you failed to attend or participate in a consultation, you can ask for a 'mandatory reconsideration' and then appeal. See Chapter 7 for more details on how to do this. Explain why you did not attend or participate and send evidence confirming this, such as a letter from your GP if you were ill. You should also make a new claim, in case the decision is not changed.

The healthcare professional's report

After the consultation, the healthcare professional writes a report for the Department for Work and Pensions (DWP), setting out your clinical and other relevant history, your own description of how your condition affects you (including your 'typical day'), her/his clinical findings and advice on which 'descriptors' you satisfy.

The report also advises on the probable timescale over which your condition is likely to affect you. This information is used by the DWP to decide whether your ability to carry out everyday activities will be affected for at least a year, the duration of your award and when you should be reassessed.

If you are refused personal independence payment or you do not receive the amount you think you should get, you can ask for a copy of the report and point out any inaccuracies. If there are significant mistakes, you can also make a complaint.

When are you reassessed?

You can be reassessed for personal independence payment at any time. This is likely to happen when you have an award of personal independence payment and:

- you report a change in your condition or needs
- the date has been reached when the healthcare professional has advised that your case should be reviewed

You must complete a different questionnaire focusing on whether your condition has changed, and are likely to be asked to attend another consultation.

If you have been refused personal independence payment in the past, you can make a new claim at any time, and are then reassessed. You should consider doing this if your condition has deteriorated and your needs have increased.

4. Getting paid

The decision on your claim

The Department for Work and Pensions (DWP) writes to you, informing you of its decision on your claim for personal independence payment. This includes the decision maker's reasoning and details of which 'descriptors' you satisfy.

The decision letter also explains how you are paid and your duty to report relevant changes in your circumstances, such as if your condition changes, or if you go into hospital or a care home.

If your claim has been refused or you think you should have been awarded a higher amount, you can ask for a 'mandatory reconsideration' and then appeal. There is more information about this in Chapter 7.

How much personal independence payment do you get?

Amount of personal independence payment (2016/17 rates)		
Component	Standard weekly rate	Enhanced weekly rate
Daily living component	£55.10	£82.30
Mobility component	£21.80	£57.45

How are you paid?

Personal independence payment can be paid into a bank account, building society, credit union or post office card account. It is normally paid every four weeks in arrears. Awards of personal independence payment on the basis of terminal illness are paid weekly in advance. If someone is acting on your behalf (an 'appointee'), your personal independence payment is paid directly to her/him.

Personal independence payment can also be paid to a third party, if the Department for Work and Pensions considers this is necessary to protect your interests.

If you have a vehicle under the Motability scheme, any mobility component paid at the enhanced rate is paid directly to Motability.

How long is personal independence payment awarded for?

- You are given a short-term fixed award of up to two years if your condition is likely to improve within that period.

- You are given a longer-term fixed award if your condition is less likely to change or might be expected to worsen.

- Awards on the basis of terminal illness are normally made for three years.

- You are given an ongoing indefinite award if your condition and needs are stable and very unlikely to change, although this only applies in a small minority of cases. Your award can still be reviewed to check that it is correct. This review normally happens at least every 10 years.

What happens at the end of your award?

If your personal independence payment award is made for two years or more, you are usually contacted one year before your award is due to end. You are asked to complete a questionnaire about the daily living and mobility activities, which asks you what has changed since your award was made. You may also need to attend another consultation. The process is similar to that as for a new claim which is explained earlier in this chapter.

If you do not return the questionnaire, or attend or participate in the consultation and you are not accepted as having a good reason, your award of personal independence payment ends. You can challenge this decision, but should also make a new claim in case your challenge is not successful.

You might not be contacted one year before your award ends, particularly if you have a shorter award and the DWP thinks that your needs are likely to have decreased. In this case, you can make a new claim for personal independence up to six months before your award ends. You should be reminded to claim again 14 weeks before your award ends, but depending on where you live you may need to consider making a new claim sooner than this, to be sure of getting a decision before your old award runs out.

Further information

CPAG's *Welfare Benefits and Tax Credits Handbook* contains detailed information about the personal independence payment claims process, with references to the legislation and the most important caselaw.
On www.gov.uk there is information about how to claim personal independence payment, and also a *PIP Handbook* giving more details of how to claim and what happens. The *PIP Assessment Guide* contains details of how assessors must carry out consultations.

Chapter 4
Meeting the assessment criteria

This chapter covers:

1. The assessment criteria and qualifying period

2. Activities, descriptors and points

3. How are the descriptors applied?

What you need to know

- Personal independence payment has two 'components' – a daily living component and a mobility component. You can qualify for one or both components, which are each paid at a standard or enhanced rate.

- To qualify for either component, you must normally satisfy the assessment criteria for at least a year.

- You are assessed on your ability to carry out 10 daily living activities and two mobility activities.

- Special rules apply if you have a terminal illness. You can qualify for personal independence payment immediately and automatically satisfy the assessment crieria for the enhanced rate of the daily living component.

1. The assessment criteria and qualifying period

Personal independence payment has two 'components' – a daily living component and a mobility component. You may qualify for one or both components.

Each component can be paid at either a standard or enhanced (higher) rate, depending on how your condition affects you. It is not your condition or disability itself that qualifies you for personal independence payment, but how it affects your ability to carry out specified activities.

You are assessed on your ability to carry out 10 daily living activities and two mobility activities.

This chapter lists the activities and explains the assessment criteria. Chapter 5 explains the daily living activities in more detail and Chapter 6 explains the mobility activities.

The qualifying period

In order to qualify for personal independence payment you must have met the assessment criteria for a particular 'component' or rate for three months before the date of your claim. You must also be likely to meet the criteria for a further nine months after the date of your claim. This is known as 'the required period condition'. The purpose of this rule is to only allow you to qualify for personal independence payment if you have a longer-term condition or disability that affects you for at least a year.

You can claim personal independence payment during the three-month qualifying period, but your entitlement cannot start until the three months have elapsed. The nine-month 'forward condition' immediately follows on from the day you first qualify.

For each day you get personal independence payment, you must still be likely to satisfy the criteria for a further nine months.

If you ask for your award to be looked at again as you think you qualify for a different component or a higher rate, you must show that you have satisfied the conditions for at least three months and are likely to satisfy them for a further nine months.

EXAMPLES

The qualifying period

John has had emphysema for many years, which greatly restricts his everyday activities. When he claims personal independence payment, he satisfies both the three-month and the nine-month qualifying periods.

Jane breaks her leg. Three months later, she claims personal independence payment. The Department for Work and Pensions (DWP) decides that, although she has satisfied the criteria for an award for three months, she is unlikely to satisfy them for a further nine months because her leg will have healed before then. She is refused personal independence payment on this basis.

Samir gets the standard rate of the daily living component. His condition deteriorates and he immediately asks for his award to be looked at again. The DWP accepts that his higher level of needs is likely to last for over a year and decides that he will qualify for the enhanced rate of both components, and his award increases from three months after his condition got worse.

When does the qualifying period not apply?

You can sometimes get personal independence payment without having to satisfy the qualifying period.

• If you claim personal independence payment on the basis of having a terminal illness, you can qualify for both 'components' straight away. You do not have to meet the three-month qualifying period or the nine-month 'forward condition'.

• If you claim personal independence payment again within two years of your previous entitlement ending (or within one year if you are over 65), you do not have to satisfy the three-month qualifying condition to requalify for the same component you were getting before, provided you have the same condition or a new condition that has developed as a result of it. You must still show that you are likely to meet the criteria for nine months starting from the date of your new claim.

- If you are transferring from disability living allowance to personal independence payment, you do not need to meet the three-month qualifying condition. You must still show that you are likely to meet the criteria for nine months starting from the date of your new claim.

EXAMPLES

Getting personal independence payment without satisfying the qualifying period

Tom has just been diagnosed with pancreatic cancer and has submitted Form DS1500 from his GP, confirming that death can be expected within six months. He is automatically entitled to the enhanced rate of the daily living component and does not have to wait until three months have elapsed to qualify for personal independence payment.

Judith was getting both components of personal independence payment, but this stopped 18 months ago when her condition went into remission. It has now flared up again and she reclaims. The Department for Work and Pensions decides that she is entitled to both components again straight away, without having to satisfy the three-month qualifying period.

(If Judith had previously only been receiving one component, she could only qualify for the other component after satisfying the criteria for three months.)

2. Activities, descriptors and points

Your entitlement to personal independence payment is assessed on your ability to carry out 10 daily living activities and two mobility activities.

What are the activities?

What the law says

Daily living activities

- preparing food
- taking nutrition
- managing therapy or monitoring a health condition
- washing and bathing
- managing toilet needs or incontinence
- dressing and undressing
- communicating verbally
- reading and understanding signs, symbols and words
- engaging with other people face to face
- making budgeting decisions

Mobility activities

- planning and following journeys
- moving around

Schedule 1 Social Security (Personal Independence Payment) Regulations 2013

What are the descriptors?

Each activity is described by a number of statements (called 'descriptors') that reflect different levels of ability to carry out the activity. Each descriptor is given a number of points. The greater the level of difficulty described, the higher the number of points.

For example, the activity 'managing toilet needs or incontinence' has six descriptors.

Managing toilet needs

Descriptor	Points
Can manage toilet needs or incontinence unaided.	0
Needs to use an aid or appliance to be able to manage toilet needs or incontinence.	2
Needs supervision or prompting to be able to manage toilet needs.	2
Needs assistance to be able to manage toilet needs.	4
Needs assistance to be able to manage incontinence of either bladder or bowel.	6
Needs assistance to be able to manage incontinence of both bladder and bowel.	8

You only score points for one descriptor under each activity. You can, however, score points for any or all of the activities.

The points you score for the daily living activities and the mobility activities are added up separately.

How many points do you need?

You must score at least eight points to qualify for either component.

- If you score eight, nine, 10 or 11 points for the daily living activities, you are entitled to the standard rate of the daily living component. If you score 12 points or more, you are entitled to the enhanced rate.

- If you score eight, nine, 10 or 11 points for the mobility activities, you are entitled to the standard rate of the mobility component. If you score 12 points or more, you are entitled to the enhanced rate.

Do you have a terminal illness?

If you claim on the basis of having a terminal illness, you are automatically entitled to the enhanced rate daily living component, without having to satisfy any of the 'descriptors'.

You are not automatically entitled to the mobility component, but you qualify if you score more than eight points on the mobility activities. The information given when your claim was made and any other evidence available is used to decide if you satisfy the criteria.

EXAMPLE

Scoring points

Pat has a physical disability and uses a wheelchair outdoors. Her condition also makes a number of daily living activities more difficult for her. For the daily living activities, she scores:

- two points for preparing food (descriptor 1(b), 'needs to use an aid or appliance to be able to either prepare or cook a simple meal')

- three points for washing and bathing (descriptor 4(e), 'needs assistance to be able to get in or out of a bath or shower')

- two points for managing toilet needs (descriptor 5(b), 'needs to use an aid or appliance to be able to manage toilet needs or incontinence')

- two points for dressing and undressing (descriptor 6(d), 'needs assistance to be able to dress or undress their lower body')

- no points for the other daily living activities, which she can manage without help

This gives her a total of nine points, which entitles her to the standard rate daily living component.

In addition, she scores 12 points for the mobility activity, moving around (descriptor 2(e), 'can stand and then move more than one metre but no more than 20 metres, either aided or unaided'). This entitles her to the enhanced rate mobility component.

3. How are the descriptors applied?

Chapter 5 has more details on the daily living activities and Chapter 6 has more details on the mobility activities. Both chapters list and examine the 'descriptors' and points under each activity.

This section covers the general rules and issues about how the descriptors are applied.

What period is used?

When deciding whether a 'descriptor' applies, a 12-month period is normally looked at. This is generally the three months before the date you claim and the nine months after. If you are already getting personal independence payment, you are assessed on any day by looking at the previous three months and the following nine months.

Does your condition fluctuate?

What the law says

Fluctuating conditions

- If one descriptor in an activity is satisfied on more than 50 per cent of the days in the 'required period', that descriptor applies.

- If two or more descriptors in the same activity are satisfied on more than 50 per cent of the days in the required period, the one that scores the highest points applies.

- If none of the descriptors in an activity are satisfied on more than 50 per cent of the days in the required period but, combined, two or more scoring descriptors are satisfied on more than 50 per cent of the days, the scoring descriptor that is satisfied on the highest proportion of the days applies.

Regulation 7 Social Security (Personal Independence Payment) Regulations 2013

If your condition or needs fluctuate, this is taken into account. Although you must satisfy the criteria over the required period of 12 months, you do not have to satisfy a particular 'descriptor' on every day of this period for it to apply.

In practice, it is often difficult to assess accurately the number of days on which you satisfy a particular descriptor. This is particularly the case when a future period is being looked at. Keeping a diary may help you identify a pattern over a period of time.

You must be 'likely' to satisfy a descriptor on any particular day. If your future condition is uncertain because, for example, you might have further treatment and the outcome of it is unknown, or because the nature or speed of your recovery is in doubt, the assessment should be based on the continuing effect of your current condition, disregarding the impact of further treatment or recovery.

The descriptors should apply on a particular day if they apply at any time during the day, unless you only have difficulty for a very small part of the day. There is no distinction between the needs you have during the day and the needs you have at night.

EXAMPLE

Fluctuating conditions

Sharmani has arthritis, which particularly affects her hands. She has had the condition for two years and it is unlikely to get better. On approximately 40 per cent of the days in the required period, her arthritis prevents her from preparing a simple meal without assistance to chop up vegetables, open packaging and carry things in the kitchen. On approximately 15 per cent of the days, her arthritis flares up so badly that she is unable to prepare any food or cook at all, and relies on someone else to make all of her meals.

Although she does not satisfy any of the individual preparing food descriptors for 50 per cent of the days, she satisfies either descriptors 1(e) ('needs assistance to either prepare or cook a simple meal') or 1(f) ('cannot prepare and cook food') on more than 50 per cent of the days in total. In these circumstances, descriptor 1(e) is awarded because it applies for the highest proportion of the days.

EXAMPLE

Fluctuating conditions

Mary has ME. She is unable to walk more than 50 metres unaided as often as she needs to stop on more than 50 per cent of the days in the required period. On the other days, when she feels stronger and less tired, she can walk over 200 metres. This situation is likely to persist for over a year.

In these circumstances, descriptor 2(c) of the moving around activity applies ('can stand and then move unaided more than 20 metres but no more than 50 metres'). This scores eight points and entitles Mary to the standard rate mobility component.

What do the terms mean?

Many of the words and phrases used in the 'descriptors' are defined in the regulations, which means that ordinary words like 'cook', 'stand', 'assistance', and 'supervision' are given specific meanings. A full list is in Appendix 2. When deciding which descriptors apply to you, check if there are any special definitions of the words used.

EXAMPLE

Meaning of terms

Henri walks with prosthetic legs. He is also an athlete who regularly runs at athletic meetings using 'blades'. He scores 12 points for mobility descriptor 2(f) ('cannot either aided or unaided stand or move more than one metre'), which entitles him to the enhanced rate of the mobility component. Although he can move around without difficulty, he is unable to 'stand' in accordance with the definition of that word, which is 'to stand upright with at least one biological foot on the ground'. If he only had one leg, however, he would be able to 'stand'.

Do you use an aid or appliance?

What the law says

Aids and appliances

An 'aid or appliance' is any device which improves, provides or replaces an impaired physical or mental function.

Regulation 2 Social Security (Personal Independence Payment) Regulations 2013

Box A
Examples of aids and appliances
- artificial limb
- walking stick
- magnifying glass
- stoma
- wheelchair
- perching stool
- special cutlery
- lightweight pots and pans
- single-lever arm taps
- shower seat
- bath rail
- commode
- raised toilet seat
- incontinence pads
- stair lift
- hoist
- monkey pole
- modified buttons
- velcro fastenings
- zip pull
- long shoe horn
- hearing aid
- electronic voice aid

Aids and appliances can include items used by people without disabilities, like an electric can opener and jar opener, if you are unable to manage without them because of your disability.

Your ability to carry out an activity is assessed as if you are using any aid or appliance you normally use, or could reasonably be expected to use. You should only be expected to use items you already have or which are widely available at low or no cost, and which you are able to use and are medically appropriate for you to use. You may, for example, be assessed as able to walk using a walking stick or cut up food with adapted cutlery.

Some of the 'descriptors' specifically refer to the need to use an aid or appliance. Although these only score one or two points, you do not score any points if you can carry out the relevant activity 'unaided'. It is therefore important to refer to the aids and appliances you need to use on your questionnaire and at your consultation.

EXAMPLE

Aids and appliances

Martha had a stroke six months ago which has left her with weakness and restricted movement down her right side. She needs to use a perching stool and spiked chopping board to prepare and cook a meal. She also needs to use a long-handled sponge to wash. She has a grab handle to enable her to get on and off the toilet, and needs to wear clothes without buttons and shoes without laces, using a grabber and a long shoe horn to enable her to dress.

Martha should score two points for the descriptors 1(b) ('needs to use an aid or appliance to be able to cook a simple meal'), 4(b) ('needs to use an aid or appliance to be able to wash or bathe), 5(b) ('needs to use an aid or appliance to manage toilet needs') and 6(b) ('needs to use an aid or appliance to dress or undress'). This entitles her to the standard rate daily living component.

Note that you can score points for the planning and following journeys activity if you need an assistance dog (a dog trained to guide or assist someone with a sensory impairment) or an orientation aid (a specialist aid designed to help disabled people follow a route safely) but do not score any points for needing other things that might count as an aid or appliance.

Do you need help from other people?

The help you need from another person to undertake an activity is taken into account. This includes if you are unable to do something without help or if you need another person to do parts of an activity for you. The 'descriptors' refer to three types of help: assistance, supervision and prompting. For most activities in the daily living assessment there is also a descriptor describing your needs if you cannot manage the activity at all, even with these kinds of help.

What the law says

Help from other people

- **'Assistance'** is 'physical intervention by another person and does not include speech'. In other words, you must require the presence of, and physical help from another person for at least some of the activity.

- **'Supervision'** is 'the continuous presence of another person for the purpose of ensuring the claimant's safety'. In other words, you must need someone with you throughout the time you are carrying out the activity to make sure you stay safe.

- **'Prompting'** is 'reminding, encouraging or explaining by another person'. You must need someone to do one or more of these things to help you complete the activity. Prompting does not necessarily involve the physical presence of another person, so someone could prompt you through a phone call.

Part 1, Schedule 1 Social Security (Personal Independence Payment) Regulations 2013

You are assessed on whether you need help, not whether you actually receive it or it is available to you. So, if you have no one to help you with an activity, but you find it a struggle and really need someone to help you, you should state the kind of help that you need and score points for the relevant descriptors.

EXAMPLE

Needing help from other people

Bettina has multiple sclerosis. She lives on her own and has no one to help her. She cooks for herself, but finds it difficult to prepare and cut up food. She mainly eats ready meals, which she heats in her microwave. She also makes sure her meals consist of small pieces, so she does not have to cut up food. She uses the shower every day, but it takes her a very long time because of her poor coordination. The same applies to her dressing and undressing. For the daily living activities she scores:

- four points for descriptor 1(e) ('needs supervision or assistance to either prepare or cook a simple meal')

- two points for descriptor 2(b)(iii) ('needs assistance to be able to cut up food')

- four points for descriptor 4(f) ('needs assistance to be able to wash their body between the shoulders and waist')

- four points for descriptor 6(e) ('needs assistance to be able to dress or undress their upper body')

This gives her a total of 14 points, and she gets the enhanced rate of the daily living component.

It may be difficult for you to recognise and admit that you need help if you are independently minded and manage on your own. However, for the purpose of your personal independence payment claim, you should do your best to identify and explain the help and support you need.

EXAMPLE

Prompting from other people

Tony has severe memory problems and depression. He regularly needs to be reminded and encouraged to cook a meal, to eat, to take his medication, to bathe and dress himself, and to deal with his finances, including planning purchases and paying bills. Relatives and friends pop in to see him or ring him nearly every day about all of these things. For the daily living activities, he scores:

- two points for descriptor 1(d) ('needs prompting to be able to either prepare or cook a simple meal')

- four points for descriptor 2(d) ('needs prompting to be able to take nutrition')

- one point for descriptor 3(b)(ii) ('needs prompting to be able to manage medication')

- two points for descriptor 4(c) ('needs prompting to be able to wash or bathe')

- two points for descriptor 6(c)(i) ('needs prompting to be able to dress or undress')

- two points for descriptor 10(b) ('needs prompting to be able to make complex budgeting decisions')

This gives him a total of 13 points and he gets to the enhanced rate daily living component.

Can you undertake an activity reliably?

In order for a 'descriptor' to apply, you must be able to undertake the relevant activity reliably.

What the law says

Reliability

You must only be assessed as able to carry out an activity at the level described by a descriptor if you can do so:

- safely – in a manner unlikely to cause harm to you or another person, either during or after the activity
- to an acceptable standard
- repeatedly – as often as is reasonably required for that particular activity
- in a reasonable time period – in no more than twice the time it would normally take a person without a disability or health condition to carry out the activity

Regulation 4(2A) and (4) Social Security (Personal Independence Payment) Regulations 2013

If you cannot complete an activity at the level described by a particular descriptor safely, to an acceptable standard, repeatedly and in a reasonable time period, you should be treated as if you cannot complete it at that level at all. If you can only carry out an activity in this way with help from another person, you should score points under the descriptors which refer to the kind of help that you need.

When considering whether you can manage something 'safely' the only consideration is how likely you are to come to harm, and not how serious it would be if it happened. This means you may score points if you would often suffer a relatively minor consequence if you did the activity without help, but not score any points if there is a smaller chance that you would suffer a very serious consequence.

In considering whether you can manage an activity to an acceptable standard, the benchmark is whether the standard you manage is 'good enough'. For example, if you can only put on very loose clothes without zips or buttons and must wear slippers as you cannot manage shoes and socks without help from someone else, this would not be dressing to an acceptable standard.

The definition of 'repeatedly' means that if you need help with an activity for part of a day, that day should count as one in which you score points for the fluctuating conditions rules explained above. The exception to this is if you only need help for a very small amount of time. For example, if your condition causes one brief dizzy spell on some days, meaning you need to sit down for a few moments to recover, you would be unlikely to score any points unless there are other effects on your ability to carry out the activities.

If you have to take frequent rests or follow a set routine, you may need an aid or help from someone else to manage activities within a reasonable time period. You should think carefully about what kind of help would allow you to manage the activity in less than twice the time someone without your condition would take.

EXAMPLES

Reliability

Frank has severe depression. He only eats soup or convenience foods if no one is around to encourage him to eat a proper meal. Descriptor 2(d) ('needs prompting to be able to take nutrition') applies because his diet without being prompted would not be taking nutrition to an acceptable standard.

Ruth can walk 20–50 metres once or twice a day using a walking stick. After this, however, she gets too tired and is in too much pain to be able to walk more than 20 metres again on the same day.

She does not satisfy mobility descriptor 2(d) ('can walk more than 20 metres but no more than 50 metres') because she cannot do so repeatedly. It would be reasonable to expect someone to be able to walk such a distance more than twice in a day. Instead, she satisfies descriptor 2(e) ('can walk more than one metre but no more than 20 metres') because she can manage this several times a day. This scores 12 points and she is entitled to the enhanced rate of the mobility component.

EXAMPLE

Reliability

Sarwan has obsessive compulsive disorder. His ritualised behaviour means it takes him several hours to complete short journeys because he only feels safe if he follows certain routes using certain buses at particular times. Help from another person would not change this, as he refuses to change his routine even if a family member is with him.

He satisfies mobility descriptor 1(e) ('cannot undertake any journey because it would cause him overwhelming psychological distress') because he is unable to complete a journey in a reasonable time without overwhelming distress. He qualifies for the mobility component at the standard rate.

What CPAG says

Applying the descriptors

CPAG is concerned that the rules for determining how the descriptors are applied are too complex, mechanistic and inflexible.

However, this system of assessing entitlement means that you score points for a descriptor if you cannot manage an activity without that kind of help 'reliably' – even if only one of the four factors is missing. You should be very clear about how you would be unsafe, how long the activity would take, whether you could manage as often as you need to and to what standard you could manage an activity without help. This should help you to make sure that the points you are given in the assessment reflect the kind of help that you need, whether you can currently get that help or not.

Further information

CPAG's *Welfare Benefits and Tax Credits Handbook* contains detailed information about the personal independence payment assessment, with references to the legislation and the most important caselaw.

On www.gov.uk there is *Advice for Decision Making*, which the Department for Work and Pensions has produced for its own staff. Chapter P2 looks at the personal independence payment assessment criteria. The *PIP Assessment Guide* (also on www.gov.uk) for healthcare professionals explains how to decide which descriptors are satisfied.

Disability Rights UK has produced a useful booklet about claiming personal independence payment, with information about the assessment criteria. You can download it at www.disabilityrightsuk.org/personal-independence-payment-pip.

Chapter 5
The daily living activities

This chapter covers:

1. Do you have difficulty preparing and cooking food?

2. Do you have difficulty eating and drinking?

3. Do you have difficulty taking medication, undergoing treatment at home, or keeping an eye on your health?

4. Do you have difficulty washing and bathing?

5. Do you have difficulty using the toilet?

6. Do you have difficulty getting dressed or undressed?

7. Do you have difficulty speaking and hearing?

8. Do you have difficulty reading?

9. Do you have difficulty spending time with other people?

10. Do you have difficulty managing money?

What you need to know

- There are 10 daily living activities in the personal independence payment assessment.

- Each activity contains a series of statements (called 'descriptors') which score a certain number of points.

- If you score at least eight points, you get the daily living component paid at the standard rate. If you score 12 points or more or you are 'terminally ill', you get the enhanced rate.

- Only the activities explained in this chapter are taken into account. Any other help you need is not counted.

What CPAG says

The daily living activities

The choice of only 10 daily living activities may make it easy for you to work out whether you are entitled or not. However, it excludes a need for help with any other aspects of daily living that may be important to you. This makes it important for you to think about your coping strategies to manage these activities, and explain the help that you need, and not just the help that you currently get when you claim.

1. Do you have difficulty preparing and cooking food?

What the law says

Activity one: preparing food

Descriptor	Points
(a) Can prepare and cook a simple meal unaided.	0
(b) Needs to use an aid or appliance to be able to either prepare or cook a simple meal.	2
(c) Cannot cook a simple meal using a conventional cooker but is able to do so using a microwave.	2
(d) Needs prompting to be able to either prepare or cook a simple meal.	2
(e) Needs supervision or assistance to either prepare or cook a simple meal.	4
(f) Cannot prepare and cook food.	8

Schedule 1, Part 2 Social Security (Personal Independence Payment) Regulations 2013

What is looked at?

This activity looks at your ability to prepare and cook a 'simple meal'.

Box A
A simple meal

A 'simple meal' is a meal for one person, made using fresh ingredients. This means that if you can only make ready meals, and cannot open tins or peel and chop vegetables, you should score some points for this activity.

You only need to be able to prepare and cook sufficient food for one person. If you have a large family and cannot lift large pans of food, or get tired chopping enough vegetables for everyone, this is not relevant. If you have a low oven and you find it difficult to bend down to use it, this is ignored when you are assessed. Only cooking tasks at waist height or above are assessed.

EXAMPLE

Problems bending down

Bert has had back problems for years. He never uses his oven as his back often spasms when he tries to bend down and, in the past, he has burned himself dropping hot food as he got it out of the oven. This is not relevant to the assessment, but his ability to use a small pan on the hob or a microwave safely is relevant.

There are many different aids that you might use to help you prepare food or cook a meal. For example, if you have problems with your hands, you may need to use an electric tin opener, an adapted vegetable peeler, single lever arm taps or lightweight pots and pans with adapted handles. If you have problems with balance, you might need a perching stool, or a slotted spoon to help you remove cooked vegetables from boiling water safely. Remember that only things that you need to use because of your health condition or disability count as aids to help you score points.

If you cannot cook on a hob because, for example, there is a risk of burns, but you can prepare the ingredients and then cook a meal using a microwave, you score two points. It is important to think

Kitchen aids

Bibi has arthritis in her hands. She cannot use a manual tin opener because she has very poor grip. Her electric tin opener counts as an aid.

Francis was given an electric tin opener for Christmas. He has mobility problems, but no problems with his hands. Because he can use a manual tin opener, his electric one does not count as an aid to help him prepare food.

about whether you are really safe when taking hot food out of a microwave – if you are not, you may score more points. Also, if you can heat up ready meals but cannot prepare food to put in a microwave, you should explain why this is. You should be awarded a different discriptor for this activity, to reflect the help that you need to prepare food.

Using a microwave

Rose can put food in and out of her microwave safely. However, she can only heat up ready meals and tinned food, and cannot prepare fresh vegetables. She is assessed as needing assistance to prepare food.

Charlie is a widower. His wife used to do the cooking so most days he eats ready meals heated in a microwave. Unless there is a reason connected to Charlie's disability that means he cannot cook a meal, he will not score any points for this activity.

If you have mental health problems, you may need to be encouraged to cook proper meals by a friend or relative. It does not matter whether the other person has to come to your house, or just phones to remind and encourage you to make a meal. The important thing is that without this help you would not be able to prepare and cook a simple meal. For example, you might just eat takeaways and snacks as you cannot motivate yourself to cook.

If you cannot cook safely because there is a serious risk to your health, you should be assessed as needing supervision when preparing or cooking food. For example, if you have epilepsy and do not get any warning of a seizure, you could be at risk of harm when chopping vegetables or handling hot food.

EXAMPLES

Preparing food reliably

Ella has chronic fatigue syndrome. On most days she can prepare herself some toast and a cup of tea. However, if she prepares and cooks a whole meal for herself from scratch, she is so exhausted that she ends up in bed for a couple of days. She cannot prepare a simple meal as often as is reasonable.

If someone else helps Ella by doing some of the tasks, she can prepare and cook meals reliably, so she is assessed as needing assistance to prepare or cook a simple meal.

Trish has obsessive compulsive disorder. She has no problem with the physical tasks needed to prepare food, but it takes her about four hours to prepare a simple meal by herself due to the amount of cleaning, organising and handwashing she does between each task. Her husband encourages her to try to modify her routines to get food ready more quickly, but still has to do a lot of the cooking to get meals ready on time. Trish cannot prepare and cook a meal within a reasonable time period and so is assessed as needing assistance to do so.

The help you need to prepare or cook food must be needed because of your health condition or disability, not just because you are not good at cooking.

If you cannot manage some cooking tasks reliably yourself (even using an aid), you could be assessed as needing assistance to prepare or cook food. If you have so many difficulties with preparing and cooking food that someone else needs to do all of the preparation and cooking for you, you should be assessed as being unable to prepare and cook food at all.

2. Do you have difficulty eating and drinking?

What the law says

Activity two: taking nutrition

Descriptor	Points
(a) Can take nutrition unaided.	0
(b) Needs–	2
(i) to use an aid or appliance to be able to take nutrition; or	
(ii) supervision to be able to take nutrition; or	
(iii) assistance to be able to cut up food.	
(c) Needs a therapeutic source to be able to take nutrition.	2
(d) Needs prompting to be able to take nutrition.	4
(e) Needs assistance to be able to manage a therapeutic source to take nutrition.	6
(f) Cannot convey food and drink to their mouth and needs another person to do so.	10

Schedule 1, Part 2 Social Security (Personal Independence Payment) Regulations 2013

What is looked at?

This activity looks at how you eat and drink, including cutting up your food, chewing and swallowing it. If you can eat independently but spill so much food that you need to change your clothes afterwards, you should score some points for this activity.

Aids that you might need include adapted cutlery or a specially designed cup with a drinking straw if you find it difficult to hold a cup or glass to your mouth without spilling its contents.

Box B
Therapeutic source

A 'therapeutic source' is defined as 'parenteral or enteral tube feeding, using a rate-limiting device such as a delivery system or feed pump'. This is when you are given food or drink through a tube going directly into either your intestines or your bloodstream, such as a peg feed, nasogastric tube, or if you get nutrition through an intravenous drip. You score more points for this activity if you need help from someone else to use the equipment.

If you are at risk of choking on food, but do not need to use a feeding tube to avoid the risk, you may be assessed as needing supervision to take nutrition, if the risk is serious enough.

If you do not eat an appropriate amount unless someone reminds you, you should be assessed as needing prompting to eat. This could be if your condition means that you overeat, or if you would not eat proper meals without encouragement. You may need encouragement to cook a proper meal and also to eat it. These are two different needs, so you can score points for both this activity and the preparing food activity above.

EXAMPLES

Prompting to eat

Fritz has dementia, and often forgets to eat unless someone visits him and reminds him to have some food.

Fritz needs prompting to eat safely.

Graham has a genetic disorder which means that he always feels hungry. He also has a learning disability and needs to be reminded to eat appropriate portions to manage his weight.

Graham needs prompting to eat safely.

The highest score for this activity is given if you need someone else to feed you and give you drinks – for example, if you have lost the use of both arms.

3. Do you have difficulty taking medication, undergoing treatment at home, or keeping an eye on your health?

What the law says

Activity three: managing therapy or monitoring a health condition

Descriptor	Points
(a) Either– (i) does not receive medication or therapy or need to monitor a health condition; or (ii) can manage medication or therapy or monitor a health condition unaided.	0
(b) Needs either– (i) to use an aid or appliance to be able to manage medication; or (ii) supervision, prompting or assistance to be able to manage medication or monitor a health condition.	1
(c) Needs supervision, prompting or assistance to be able to manage therapy that takes no more than 3.5 hours a week.	2
(d) Needs supervision, prompting or assistance to be able to manage therapy that takes more than 3.5 but no more than seven hours a week.	4
(e) Needs supervision, prompting or assistance to be able to manage therapy that takes more than seven but no more than 14 hours a week.	6
(f) Needs supervision, prompting or assistance to be able to manage therapy that takes more than 14 hours a week.	8

Schedule 1, Part 2 Social Security (Personal Independence Payment) Regulations 2013

What is looked at?

This activity looks at the help you need with your medication or treatment at home, and whether you can detect changes in your condition which could be dangerous and take the necessary action. Only help that you need with medication taken or therapy carried out at home that has been prescribed or recommended by a doctor or other health professional counts.

An aid to help you take medication could be a special dosing pack that helps you take the right medicines at the right time, or a mobile phone alarm to remind you to take your tablets if you have memory problems. However, syringes and inhalers are not aids – they are the way you take your medicine and do not improve or replace a physical or mental function.

If you are at risk of taking an overdose or you have epilepsy and may need emergency medication if you have a seizure, you may be assessed as needing supervision to manage your medication or monitor your health. If you cannot take your medicine without help from someone else, you also score points. This could apply if you cannot open a pill bottle without help, for example.

Box C

Medication and therapy

'Therapy' is anything to help with your condition that you have been told to do at home by your doctor or another health professional, if your condition would worsen if you do not do it. It includes physiotherapy exercises to build up your muscles, dialysis treatment and massage. You must need help with the therapy from another person to score points. There is no clear dividing line between what counts as 'medication' and 'therapy'. For example, if you are prescribed a cream for severe eczema this would count as 'medication'. However, if you have problems with your hands and arms so cannot apply it yourself, someone else applying the cream for you may count as 'assistance to manage therapy'.

EXAMPLE

Supervision to take medication

Helen has severe depression and a history of suicide attempts. She needs supervision to take her medication, because she would be likely to take an overdose if someone was not there to check that she takes the right dose.

Although the assessment normally looks at your needs on different days, the descriptors in this activity concern how long you need help with therapy for during a week. You are assessed as needing help with therapy on all the days in a week, irrespective of how the therapy is spread throughout the week. For example, if you need help with home dialysis, which you do three times a week, you are assessed as needing assistance with therapy on every day of a week in which you do the dialysis at home.

The periods of time mentioned refer to how long you need help for, not to how long your therapy takes overall. If you need help to set up a machine that is needed for your therapy, time someone else spends helping you with that also counts, even if you do not need any more help once the machine is set up.

EXAMPLE

Help with therapy

Imran had a stroke last year. He is regaining his speech and motor function slowly but has to do stretching exercises for half an hour a day and an hour of speech therapy. His partner helps with both of these. Imran should be assessed as needing assistance with therapy for between seven and 14 hours a week, as long as his treatment is expected to last for at least a year.

---

4. Do you have difficulty washing and bathing?

What the law says

Activity four: washing and bathing

Descriptor	Points
(a) Can wash and bathe unaided.	0
(b) Needs to use an aid or appliance to be able to wash or bathe.	2
(c) Needs supervision or prompting to be able to wash or bathe.	2
(d) Needs assistance to be able to wash either their hair or body below the waist.	2
(e) Needs assistance to be able to get in or out of a bath or shower.	3
(f) Needs assistance to be able to wash their body between the shoulders and waist.	4
(g) Cannot wash and bathe at all and needs another person to wash their entire body.	8

Schedule 1, Part 2 Social Security (Personal Independence Payment) Regulations 2013

What is looked at?

This activity looks at the help you need to keep clean. Most of the descriptors focus on having a bath or shower.

Aids that you might need to use include a bath lift, a shower seat so you do not need to stand up all of the time, or grab rails in the shower to help you get in and out. If you have mental health problems and need to be encouraged to keep yourself clean, you should score points for this activity if someone phones to persuade you to have a bath or shower, for example.

If you need someone to keep an eye on you while you are in the bath or shower (for example, because you are at risk of falls or have uncontrolled epilepsy), you may be assessed as needing supervision to bathe.

If you would need help from someone else to get into an unadapted bath, you should score points for needing assistance to do so, even if you actually have a wet room or grab rails fitted that mean you manage at home without anyone else to help you.

EXAMPLES

Washing and bathing

Neil has an autistic spectrum disorder. He can wash himself, but is obsessed with water and so stays in the bath for hours unless encouraged to get out by his support worker. He needs prompting to be able to bathe in a reasonable time.

Kerry finds it hard to wash her legs as she has trouble bending down due to back problems. Her husband normally helps her to do this. She needs assistance to wash her body below the waist.

5. Do you have difficulty using the toilet?

What the law says

Activity five: managing toilet needs or incontinence

Descriptor	Points
(a) Can manage toilet needs or incontinence unaided.	0
(b) Needs to use an aid or appliance to be able to manage toilet needs or incontinence.	2
(c) Needs supervision or prompting to be able to manage toilet needs.	2
(d) Needs assistance to be able to manage toilet needs.	4
(e) Needs assistance to be able to manage incontinence of either bladder or bowel.	6
(f) Needs assistance to be able to manage incontinence of both bladder and bowel.	8

Schedule 1, Part 2 Social Security (Personal Independence Payment) Regulations 2013

What is looked at?

Box D
Toilet needs and managing incontinence

This activity looks at very specific areas in which you might need help. 'Toilet needs' means:

- getting on and off an unadapted toilet
- using the toilet
- cleaning yourself afterwards

Even if you only need an aid or help from someone else with one of these three aspects you should still score some points.

'Manage incontinence' means to deal with continence problems of the bladder or bowel, including using a collecting device like a pad or catheter, and to clean yourself afterwards.

Any other difficulties, such as undressing to go to the toilet or getting dressed afterwards, are not considered.

A commode can count as an aid, but only if you need it due to continence problems, and not if you use it as you need help to get upstairs to your bathroom during the day, for example. Other examples of aids to manage your toilet needs are a bidet or bottom wiper if you find it hard to clean yourself, or a raised toilet seat or grab rails to help you use the toilet safely. Incontinence pads and stomas or catheters are examples of aids to help with continence.

You score more points if you need physical help from another person, for example, with wiping yourself or getting up from the toilet. If you use a catheter or a collecting bag and need help with this from another person, you are assessed as needing help with managing incontinence. You score more points if you need help with incontinence of both your bladder and bowel.

6. Do you have difficulty getting dressed or undressed?

What the law says

Activity six: dressing and undressing

Descriptor	Points
(a) Can dress and undress unaided.	0
(b) Needs to use an aid or appliance to be able to dress or undress.	2
(c) Needs either–	2
(i) prompting to be able to dress, undress or determine appropriate circumstances for remaining clothed; or	
(ii) prompting or assistance to be able to select appropriate clothing.	
(d) Needs assistance to be able to dress or undress their lower body.	2
(e) Needs assistance to be able to dress or undress their upper body.	4
(f) Cannot dress or undress at all.	8

Schedule 1, Part 2 Social Security (Personal Independence Payment) Regulations 2013

What is looked at?

Aids for this activity include things to help you dress, such as a long shoe horn, and grabbers for your socks. If you have to wear clothing that makes it easier to dress without help, such as velcro fastenings, large buttons, front-fastening bras, zips and loose-fitting clothing, this counts as an aid to help you dress if you need it because of your health condition or disability, but not if you just prefer to wear these kind of clothes. However, if you need to be reminded or helped to dress in clothes that are appropriate for your culture or religion, you should score points for this. You may also score points if your behaviour is disinhibited because of cognitive or mental health problems, and this means you are likely to undress in public unless encouraged to keep your clothes on.

You may need someone to tell you what to wear. For example, this might be because you have a visual impairment and cannot see whether clothes are dirty, or because you have a learning disability and do not remember to dress warmly in winter.

Your ability to put on or take off shoes and socks is also looked at. If you need help to get your shoes on without help, this counts as assistance with dressing the lower body.

You score more points if you need help to dress your upper body. If someone has to help you put on all your clothes, you are assessed as being unable to dress at all.

EXAMPLE

Dressing and undressing

Nadja is registered blind. She can dress herself but needs someone to tell her whether her clothes are clean, so she is assessed as needing prompting to dress.

After being awarded personal independence payment, she has a stroke and this leaves her left arm and leg almost completely paralysed. She is very determined and can still dress herself, but this takes her almost an hour if there is no one to help her. This is not a reasonable time to take getting dressed, so she is assessed as being unable to dress at all. It does not matter whether or not there is anyone to help her get dressed; the important point is the difficulty she has with this activity.

7. Do you have difficulty speaking and hearing?

What the law says

Activity seven: communicating verbally

Descriptor	Points
(a) Can express and understand verbal information unaided.	0
(b) Needs to use an aid or appliance to be able to speak or hear.	2
(c) Needs communication support to be able to express or understand complex verbal information.	4
(d) Needs communication support to be able to express or understand basic verbal information.	8
(e) Cannot express or understand verbal information at all even with communication support.	12

Schedule 1, Part 2 Social Security (Personal Independence Payment) Regulations 2013

What is looked at?

This activity looks at your ability to speak and hear. If you need an interpreter to communicate in English, this does not mean that you score any points for this activity, unless you also have problems speaking or understanding your first language.

Aids that might help you to speak or hear are hearing aids or an electronic voice aid if you are unable to speak.

If you need 'communication support' from another person, the number of points you score depends on what you need help with. If you can only say or understand a simple sentence without help, you are assessed as needing help with 'complex verbal information'. If you need help even to say or understand simple sentences, like 'I live in London' or 'I need the toilet', you are assessed as needing help with 'basic verbal information'. For example, if you do not have this kind of help and communicate by writing things down, you should be assessed as needing the kind of help that would allow you to communicate verbally. You are awarded most points if you cannot communicate verbally at all, even with support from someone who knows you well.

> Box E
> **Communication support**
>
> If you need help from another person to communicate verbally, it must fit within the definition of 'communication support' for you to score any points. The person helping you must either be trained in communicating with someone with your needs, such as a British Sign Language interpreter, or experienced in communicating with you, such as a relative or close friend who understands your speech more easily than strangers.

If your condition makes you very anxious in social situations, it is only possible for you to score points for this activity if your condition affects the function of speaking or hearing, and not if you are reluctant to speak due to shyness, for example. If you are unable to speak reliably due to a mental health condition or cognitive impairment, you should make this very clear when claiming.

EXAMPLES

Communicating verbally

Ian has been profoundly deaf since birth. He cannot speak at all, but is fluent in British Sign Language. He is assessed as needing communication support to express basic verbal information.

Sanjay has a mild speech impediment, and occasionally people who do not know him well have to ask him to repeat himself. This makes him quite shy, especially around people he does not know well. He is assessed as being able to express and understand verbal communication unaided, as he does not need specialist help to talk to people he does not know well. If his speech impediment were more serious, he might score points in the assessment.

8. Do you have difficulty reading?

What the law says

Activity eight: reading and understanding signs, symbols and words

Descriptor	Points
(a) Can read and understand basic and complex written information either unaided or using spectacles or contact lenses.	0
(b) Needs to use an aid or appliance, other than spectacles or contact lenses, to be able to read or understand either basic or complex written information.	2
(c) Needs prompting to be able to read or understand complex written information.	2
(d) Needs prompting to be able to read or understand basic written information.	4
(e) Cannot read or understand signs, symbols or words at all.	8

Schedule 1, Part 2 Social Security (Personal Independence Payment) Regulations 2013

What is looked at?

This activity looks at the problems you have reading. If you cannot read English, but can read another language without any problems, you do not score any points. If you need to use glasses or contact lenses to read but have no other problems reading, you do not score any points. If you can only read Braille, you are assessed as not able to read at all.

Aids that you may need to help you read include a magnifying glass, or a letter reader that magnifies text. When deciding how many points you score, your ability to read using aids like these both inside and outside your home is considered. This means that you may be able to score points for this activity if you only have problems in the dark or very bright light, depending on how serious your problems reading in these conditions are, and how often you are affected.

EXAMPLE

Reading with an aid

Roxanne is partially sighted and uses a specialist magnifier at home to understand the content of letters. The Department for Work and Pensions (DWP) assesses her as needing an aid or appliance to read, because it decides she could use a magnifying glass when out of the house. She asks for the decision to be looked at again and explains that her vision is so poor that she cannot use a magnifying glass for bus timetables or labels on items in shops. The DWP agrees and changes her award to discriptor 8(c) ('needs prompting to be able to read complex written information').

If you can read words, but do not understand the information and need someone to explain what it means, you score points in this activity. You score more points if you need help understanding 'basic written information', which means things like street signs, dates and numbers. If you can understand these things but need help with reading sentences, you are assessed as needing help to understand 'complex written information'.

EXAMPLES

Help with reading

Sebastian has Down's syndrome. He can read very simple stories if someone explains what some of the words mean, but needs help to understand official letters or recipes. He is assessed as needing prompting to understand complex written information.

Tina is registered blind. She is an academic and author of several books. However, as she has completely lost her sight and can only read Braille, she is assessed as unable to read.

9. Do you have difficulty spending time with other people?

What the law says

Activity nine: engaging with other people face to face

Descriptor	Points
(a) Can engage with other people unaided.	0
(b) Needs prompting to be able to engage with other people.	2
(c) Needs social support to be able to engage with other people.	4
(d) Cannot engage with other people due to such engagement causing either–	8
(i) overwhelming psychological distress to the claimant; or	
(ii) the claimant to exhibit behaviour which would result in a substantial risk of harm to the claimant or another person.	

Schedule 1, Part 2 Social Security (Personal Independence Payment) Regulations 2013

What is looked at?

This activity looks at whether you can behave appropriately in social situations, understand other people's body language and feelings, and form friendships. Some people are less comfortable in social situations than others. To score points for this activity, your problems with social interaction must be caused by a physical or mental condition, rather than your personal preference. It may be that a physical health problem (such as continence problems or a severe skin condition) makes you worried about meeting other people. If this makes you so anxious that you need help from another person to meet others, you should score some points for this activity.

Box F
Social support

If you need help from either a trained professional or someone who knows you very well to manage in social situations, you are assessed as needing 'social support'. It is not necessary that a professional who you get this kind of support from is always with you. What is important is that the support you get allows you to engage with other people, and you would not be able to do so without that help. Similarly, if you normally get help from a family member who knows you very well, for this to count as being 'social support' there must be a reason that encouragement from someone you do not know well would not allow you to engage with other people.

If you need some extra help, but not necessarily from a professional or someone who knows you very well, you are assessed as needing 'prompting' rather than social support, and you score fewer points for this activity.

EXAMPLES

Social support and prompting

Ursula has anxiety and severe depression. She has lost touch with most of her friends, and only feels comfortable around her closest friend and her sister. She is able to spend some time with other people she knows less well, but only if one of them is there to support her. Her sister and closest friend have got used to helping her manage over the past couple of years. Even though neither has any formal training, Ursula is assessed as needing social support to engage with other people.

Violet also has depression. Her friends noticed that she was not turning up when they had arranged to meet. They now make sure that someone calls Violet a few hours beforehand to encourage her to come along, and this means that Violet is able to stay in touch and is much less isolated. Violet needs prompting to engage with other people.

If you are not normally able to interact with others, even with the help of a relative or a professional, you score more points. Your problems must be due to how upset you get by this, or there being a risk of harm to you or someone else as a result of your behaviour around other people.

Engaging with people face to face

Maurice has an autistic spectrum disorder and complex learning disabilities. He cannot go out of the house without his support worker, as he needs to be constantly reminded of the need to respect other people's personal space. Even with the help of his support worker (he gets one-to-one support 24 hours a day), he has never been able to establish close friendships. Maurice is assessed as unable to engage with other people at all.

10. Do you have difficulty managing money?

What the law says

Activity 10: making budgeting decisions

Descriptor	Points
(a) Can manage complex budgeting decisions unaided.	0
(b) Needs prompting or assistance to be able to make complex budgeting decisions.	2
(c) Needs prompting or assistance to be able to make simple budgeting decisions.	4
(d) Cannot make any budgeting decisions at all.	6

Schedule 1, Part 2 Social Security (Personal Independence Payment) Regulations 2013

What is looked at?

This activity looks at your ability to manage money. You are assessed as needing help with 'complex budgeting decisions' if someone needs to help you manage your household bills. If you need help to work out simple sums, such as how much change you should be given in a shop, or adding together the prices of things to work out how much money you need, you are assessed as needing help with 'simple budgeting decisions'.

If you cannot add or subtract or you do not understand the value of money, you are assessed as being unable to make budgeting decisions at all.

EXAMPLES

Making budgeting decisions

Ildiko has bipolar disorder. Although she was very good at maths at school, when she is feeling high she often spends all her money on large and inappropriate presents or ideas for starting a new business, and does not have anything left for her bills or to buy food. If she is feeling low, she ignores the bills unless her brother encourages her to pay them. She is assessed as needing prompting to make complex budgeting decisions.

Conrad has a learning disability. He can do simple addition, but often needs to be reminded to think about how much money he has by his support worker when they are shopping, and cannot calculate change. He is assessed as needing prompting to make simple budgeting decisions.

Further information

CPAG's *Welfare Benefits and Tax Credits Handbook* contains detailed information about the personal independence payment daily living activities, with references to the legislation and the most important caselaw.
On www.gov.uk there is *Advice for Decision Making*, which the Department for Work and Pensions has produced for its own staff. Chapter P2 ends with an explanation of how the government thinks that the daily living activities should be interpreted. The

PIP Assessment Guide (also on www.gov.uk) explains to the healthcare professionals how to decide which of the descriptors you satisfy.
Disability Rights UK has produced a useful booklet about claiming personal independence payment, with information about how to explain your problems with the different daily living activities on the assessment questionnaire. You can download it at www.disabilityrightsuk.org/personal-independence-payment-pip.

Chapter 6
The mobility activities

This chapter covers:

1. Do you have difficulty planning or following journeys?

2. Do you have difficulty walking?

What you need to know

- There are two mobility activities in the personal independence payment assessment.

- Each activity contains a series of statements (called 'descriptors') which score a certain number of points.

- If you score at least eight points, you get the mobility component, paid at the standard rate. If you score 12 points or more, you get the enhanced rate.

- Only the activities explained in this chapter are taken into account. Any other help you need is not counted.

What CPAG says

The mobility activites

The two mobility activities are both confusingly written, so it can be hard to work out which rate you should qualify for. This also means that there are lots of cases from the Upper Tribunal explaining how these activities should be interpreted. The information in this chapter may be overtaken by future decisions on how to apply the criteria.

CPAG recommends that you try to get help from a specialist benefits adviser to help you decide which points you should score for the mobility component.

1. Do you have difficulty planning or following journeys?

What the law says

Activity one: planning and following journeys

Descriptor	Points
(a) Can plan and follow the route of a journey unaided.	0
(b) Needs prompting to be able to undertake any journey to avoid overwhelming psychological distress to the claimant.	4
(c) Cannot plan the route of a journey.	8
(d) Cannot follow the route of an unfamiliar journey without another person, assistance dog or orientation aid.	10
(e) Cannot undertake any journey because it would cause overwhelming psychological distress to the claimant.	10
(f) Cannot follow the route of a familiar journey without another person, an assistance dog or an orientation aid.	12

Schedule 1, Part 3 Social Security (Personal Independence Payment) Regulations 2013

What is looked at?

This activity looks at your ability to work out and follow the route of a journey. If you need encouragement to go out or cannot go out at all most days, you also score points for this activity.

'Psychological distress' means distress related to an enduring mental health condition or an intellectual or cognitive impairment. Your mental health condition may have an underlying physical cause. For example, you may have unmanageable incontinence which means you are anxious about making journeys outside the home. If this

Box A
Help to follow journeys

An 'assistance dog' is a dog trained to guide or assist a person with a sensory impairment.

'Orientation aids' are specialist aids designed to assist disabled people following a route, such as a long white cane. If you use something like a smartphone app to help you, whether it counts as an orientation aid or not depends on whether it is designed to help someone with your condition or not.

'Another person' is not defined, but the other person must be helping you to 'follow the route', or, to put it another way, to navigate the path of your journey.

'Prompting' is someone reminding or encouraging you to go out, even if they only do this by telephone. However, the help must be needed to get you out of the house.

anxiety is diagnosed as a separate condition and is so severe that you cannot go out on most days, you score sufficient points to qualify for the standard rate of the mobility component.

Psychological distress can also be relevant to your ability to 'follow the route' of a journey, if you get so upset that you can no longer follow a route and need another person to help you with this. However, if the other person only provides you with reassurance or encouragement, then you are likely to be assessed as needing 'prompting' instead, and score fewer points.

Unexpected changes to the environment, such as roadworks and changed bus stops, are commonplace problems with navigating that you may encounter, so think about whether you could manage if such disruption occurred. If you could not manage to find an alternative route without help, you should be assessed as needing another person to follow the route of a journey. How many points you score depends on whether you would have problems with all journeys, or just unfamiliar ones.

If you cannot plan the route of a journey, for example due to a cognitive impairment, you qualify for the standard rate of the mobility component even if you could follow a journey that someone else has planned for you without any problems.

Planning and following journeys

Lukas has anxiety and depression. Due to his mental health problems, he does not go out at all most days, even if someone comes round and offers to go out with him. He is assessed as being unable to undertake any journey. He scores 10 points and gets the standard rate mobility component.

Veronique has a visual impairment. She uses a long white cane whenever she is out, including to get to her local shops or pick up her children from their primary school. She is assessed as needing an orientation aid to follow a familiar journey. She scores 12 points and is entitled to the enhanced rate mobility component.

2. Do you have difficulty walking?

What is looked at?

This activity looks at your ability to walk without severe discomfort, such as breathlessness, pain or fatigue. It distinguishes between your ability to stand and then walk up to 20 metres, up to 50 metres, up to 200 metres and over 200 metres. If you have a psychosomatic condition that makes you believe you cannot walk far, you can score points for this activity, as long as your walking is restricted enough, even if no one can find anything physically wrong with you.

When you are working out the distance you can manage, remember that the assessment looks at what you can manage 'reliably'. This means safely, to an acceptable standard, repeatedly and in a

What the law says

Activity two: moving around

Descriptor	Points
(a) Can stand and then move more than 200 metres, either aided or unaided.	0
(b) Can stand and then move more than 50 metres but no more than 200 metres, either aided or unaided.	4
(c) Can stand and then move unaided more than 20 metres but no more than 50 metres.	8
(d) Can stand and then move using an aid or appliance more than 20 metres but no more than 50 metres.	10
(e) Can stand and then move more than one metre but no more than 20 metres, either aided or unaided.	12
(f) Cannot, either aided or unaided, (i) stand; or (ii) move more than one metre.	12

Schedule 1, Part 3 Social Security (Personal Independence Payment) Regulations 2013

reasonable time period. This means that you should think about the manner in which you are able to walk – your gait, your speed, the risk of falls and any symptoms or side effects that could affect your ability to walk any distance, such as pain, breathlessness and fatigue.

Your ability to walk is judged on the type of surface you would normally expect outdoors, such as pavements and whether or not you can manage kerbs. Remember, it is your ability to walk on flat ground, not on uneven ground or up and down hills, that is assessed.

If you need to use an aid such as a walking stick or crutches to manage more than 50 metres reliably, you should argue that you satisfy descriptor (c) above, no matter how far you can manage using a walking aid, as the descriptor specifically looks at your ability

Box B
Aided/unaided and standing

'**Aided**' means either that you use an aid, such as crutches, a walking stick or a prosthetic limb, or that another person helps you to walk.

'**Stand**' is defined as standing upright with at least one biological foot on the ground, with or without suitable aids. A prosthetic leg is considered an aid, so if you have had some or all of one leg amputated, you are considered able to stand. If you have had both legs amputated, you are assessed as unable to stand.

'**Stand and then move**' means to be able to stand and then move independently while remaining standing. If you can stand but then you have to transfer into a wheelchair to be able to move any distance, you cannot 'stand and then move' that distance for the purpose of this activity.

'unaided' – without using any aids or getting help from someone else. However, the Department for Work and Pensions may not agree with this interpretation, and you may need to challenge the decision on your entitlement.

EXAMPLE

Stand and then move unaided

Harbajhan has chronic obstructive pulmonary disease. He can walk about 50 metres before needing a break and then manage that distance again a few more times most days, but after the first 25 metres or so he gets extreme shortness of breath and pain in his chest. He is assessed as being able to stand and then move unaided more than 20 metres, but no more than 50 metres. He scores eight points and is entitled to the standard rate mobility component.

EXAMPLES

Moving around

Clare has advanced multiple sclerosis. She can manage to stand from her bedside and go to the bathroom next door using a walking frame, but she cannot go any further without transferring to a wheelchair. She is assessed as being able to move more than one metre but no more than 20 metres, either aided or unaided. She scores 12 points and is entitled to the enhanced rate mobility component.

Sophie has emphysema and gets out of breath after about 150 metres if she tries to walk too quickly. However, if she paces herself, she can walk over a mile, taking a short pause every 400 metres or so. She is assessed as able to walk over 200 metres reliably. She scores no points for the moving around activity.

Further information

CPAG's *Welfare Benefits and Tax Credits Handbook* contains detailed information about the personal independence payment mobility activities, with references to the legislation and the most important caselaw.

On www.gov.uk there is *Advice for Decision Making*, which the Department for Work and Pensions has produced for its own staff. Chapter P2 ends with an explanation of how the government thinks that the mobility activities should be interpreted. The *PIP Assessment Guide* (also on www.gov.uk) explains to the healthcare professionals how to decide which of the descriptors you satisfy.

Disability Rights UK has produced a useful booklet about claiming personal independence payment, with information about how to explain your problems with the different mobility activities on the assessment questionnaire. You can download it at www.disabilityrightsuk.org/personal-independence-payment-pip.

Chapter 7
Challenging and changing decisions

This chapter covers:

1. What can you do if you disagree with a decision?

2. What happens if your circumstances change?

3. Have you been overpaid?

What you need to know

- If you disagree with a decision on your personal independence payment claim, you can challenge it. You must first ask the Department for Work and Pensions (DWP) for a 'mandatory reconsideration'. If you are still unhappy, you can appeal to an independent tribunal.

- If your health condition or disability gets worse, you should notify the DWP so your entitlement can be reviewed. You may be entitled to a higher amount of personal independence payment.

- If you are paid more personal independence payment than you are entitled to, the DWP considers this to be an overpayment, and you may have to repay the money.

1. What can you do if you disagree with a decision?

If you disagree with a decision, you can challenge it. You must first ask for a 'mandatory reconsideration' (the law referes to this as requesting a 'revision' of the decision). If you are still unhappy, you can appeal.

What the law says

Mandatory reconsiderations

You must ask for a revision before you can appeal. The Department for Work and Pensions (DWP) calls a revision a 'mandatory reconsideration'. If you ask for an appeal first, the DWP treats it as a request for a revision.

Regulation 7 Universal Credit, Personal Independence Payment, Jobseeker's Allowance and Employment and Support Allowance (Decisions and Appeals) Regulations 2013

How do you ask for a mandatory reconsideration?

When the Department for Work and Pensions (DWP) makes a decision on your claim for personal independence payment, it must inform you of this in writing. The decision letter should explain why the decision was made. If you disagree with the decision, you can request a 'mandatory reconsideration'. You can also ask for a further explanation of the decision by phoning the DWP on the number provided, but you do not have to do this before requesting a mandatory reconsideration. You can request a mandatory reconsideration in writing or by phone. State clearly that you are requesting a mandatory reconsideration.

Try to give a full explanation of why you think the decision is wrong by, for example, explaining where you think you should have scored sufficient points in the assessment. If you make your request by phone, it is a good idea to put it in writing as well, confirming what was said.

You must ask for a mandatory reconsideration within one month of the date of the decision. This is the date on the letter the DWP sends you. To avoid your application being late, make sure you send your request in writing within the time limit, and phone as well if your letter might arrive outside the time limit to make sure your request is registered on time.

The more information you can supply to support your case, the better the chance you have of getting the decision changed. In particular, make sure you send any further evidence you have from your GP, hospital specialist or other health professional that supports your claim. Someone from the DWP may contact you to ask for further information about why you disagree with the decision. It may be helpful if you can provide further information, but do not feel pressured into agreeing with parts of the decision that you think are wrong. At the end of the call, you should be very clear that you still want your mandatory reconsideration request to be considered.

The DWP looks at your arguments and any further evidence you send, and then issues you with a notice (known as a 'mandatory reconsideration notice'), telling you whether or not the decision has been changed.

What CPAG says

Mandatory reconsiderations

The requirement to request a mandatory reconsideration before being allowed to appeal to an independent tribunal can cause delays and confusion. You may get a phone call from the DWP after you ask for a mandatory reconsideration. You may be given an explanation or asked about the effects on your condition.

CPAG suggests that:
- even if you request a mandatory reconsideration by phone, you confirm it in writing as well
- if the DWP phones you, be very clear at the end of the call that you still want your request to be considered
- if someone is helping you to challenge the decision, you could ask the DWP to phone her/him instead

Have you missed the time limit?

If you do not request a mandatory reconsideration within the one-month time limit, you may still be able to make a late request, provided you make your request within 14 months of the original decision.

For your request to be accepted, it must clearly identify the decision you are challenging (quote the date of the decision letter to identify it) and explain fully why it was not possible for you to meet the one-month time limit. It is always best to make a late request in writing to ensure you get across all of your points. You should include the reasons why you think the decision you are challenging is wrong, and any further evidence you have to support your case. However, do not wait to get evidence to make a late request, as the later you apply, the less likely your request is to be considered.

EXAMPLE

Missed time limit

Steve has anxiety and agoraphobia. He applies for personal independence payment, but is turned down for both components. He relies on his daughter to help him deal with his post and she is away on holiday when the decision notice arrives. By the time she is back, the one-month deadline for challenging the decision has passed. With the help of his daughter, Steve writes a letter to the Department for Work and Pensions, asking for a late mandatory reconsideration. In the letter he explains why he was not able to meet the deadline, and his daughter includes a note and a copy of her flight confirmations to support this. Steve also attaches a copy of a letter from his psychiatrist, confirming his difficulties, which he did not have when he first applied.

How do you appeal?

If the decision on your personal independence payment claim has been reconsidered and you are still unhappy, you can appeal to a tribunal, which is independent of the Department for Work and Pensions (DWP). Use Form SSCS1 which is available online at www.justice.gov.uk or at www.gov.uk, or you can get a copy from your local citizens advice bureau or other advice agency.

You must appeal within one month of the date on your mandatory reconsideration notice. This time limit can be extended by up to a year if special circumstances prevented you from appealing within a month. However, it is best to appeal before the one-month deadline if you can, as it can be much harder if you have to make a late appeal.

Send Form SSCS1 directly to HM Courts and Tribunals Service, not to the DWP. The address is on the form.

Even if you have not got Form SSCS1, do not delay making your appeal. Write to HM Courts and Tribunals Service and include all the information and documents listed in Box A.

> Box A
> **Appeal checklist**
>
> Your appeal must be signed and include:
>
> - a copy of your 'mandatory reconsideration notice'
> - your name and address
> - the address where documents relating to your appeal can be sent or delivered (usually either your own address, or that of your representative if you have one)
> - the reasons why you think the decision is wrong – give as much detail as you can about why the decision is wrong, such as where you think you should have scored points in the assessment
> - whether or not you want to attend a hearing of your appeal
> - if your appeal is outside the one-month time limit, an explanation of why it is late
> - the name and address of your representative if you have one; this authorises the DWP to deal with that person about your appeal

You can choose either to attend a hearing of your appeal or to have it decided 'on the papers'. If you choose for your appeal to be decided 'on the papers', you do not have to attend a hearing and the decision is based on the written information that you and the DWP provide.

What CPAG says

Appeal hearings

Statistics show that you have a much greater chance of success if you attend an appeal hearing. This can be an intimidating idea, but if you can get a representative, or even a friend or relative, to accompany you, this may help to make the experience less stressful.

If you choose to attend a hearing, the tribunal panel has the opportunity to ask you questions in person (but cannot perform a medical examination). The panel usually comprises three members, one of whom has legal training. Although it can be daunting to attend an appeal hearing, it is advisable to choose this option if you can because your chances of success are greater. Your representative can go with you. If you opt to attend a hearing, you are sent a date and details of the venue.

You do not have to name a representative, but it can be a good idea. The appeal process can be confusing and stressful, and your chances of success are generally better if you have an 'expert' to help you. This could be an adviser from a citizens advice bureau or other welfare rights service, or a friend or relative who has good knowledge of social security matters.

Once HM Courts and Tribunals Service receives your SSCS1 form or appeal letter, it notifies the DWP, which then has 28 days in which to respond. A copy of this response is sent to you, or to your representative if you have one. This includes a copy of your claim form, a full statement of the reasons for the decision and references to the social security law on which the DWP is relying.

EXAMPLE

Appeals

Steve's late request for a mandatory reconsideration is accepted, but when he receives his 'mandatory reconsideration notice' it says that the decision has not been changed and that he is still not entitled to any personal independence payment. He decides to appeal and approaches a local welfare rights service for help. An adviser visits him at home to help him complete Form SSCS1 and agrees to be his representative. Steve chooses to attend a hearing, and the representative arranges a taxi to the hearing and makes sure Steve's daughter is free to accompany him. At the hearing, Steve gives a full explanation of the help he needs, and he is awarded the personal independence payment mobility component.

2. What happens if your circumstances change?

If your health condition or disability changes, you should inform the Department for Work and Pensions (DWP) as soon as possible, either by phone or in writing. It is best to do this in writing if you can, and keep a copy of the letter for your records. If you phone, make sure you note the date and time of your call and keep a record of what was said.

The DWP reviews your personal independence payment award (called a 'supersession') to decide whether it needs to be adjusted to take account of your new circumstances.

It is in your interest to notify the DWP if your condition worsens, as this could mean that you are entitled to a higher amount of personal independence payment. However, remember that you must report any change in your circumstances that might affect your entitlement, including if your condition improves. If you do not tell the DWP and the DWP subsequently becomes aware of the change and adjusts your award at a later date, you may have been overpaid and may have to pay some money back.

If the DWP thinks you have been overpaid because you have not reported a relevant change in your circumstances, you may be considered to have acted fraudulently. This could lead to a criminal conviction or a penalty, and your personal independence payment could be suspended for a set period. You should therefore report immediately any change in your circumstances that might affect your entitlement. If you are not certain whether a change in your circumstances is relevant, you should report it. If you are accused of fraud or invited to an 'interview under caution', you should get specialist legal advice as soon as you can.

In addition to the regular scheduled reviews of your personal independence payment award, the DWP can also review your award if it believes that there may have been a relevant change in your circumstances.

As part of the review process, you must complete a new assessment questionnaire, and may have to attend another consultation. Provide as much evidence as possible of your current needs, such as a letter from your GP, hospital reports and details of your medication.

If you disagree with the decision following the review, you can ask for a mandatory reconsideration, and then appeal to a tribunal if necessary.

What CPAG says

Changes of circumstances

The rules say that you must inform the DWP of any changes that you are specifically asked to report, so check letters about your award. You also have to report any other changes that you should know might affect your personal independence payment, which could include if:
- the effect of your condition worsens
- the effect of your condition improves
- you stop receiving treatment
- you go into hospital or residential care
- you change your address or leave the UK

If you are in any doubt about whether a change is relevant, you should seek advice.

EXAMPLE

Change of circumstances

Joe is partially sighted and gets the personal independence allowance standard rate daily living component. His vision gradually worsens, to the point where he has lost his sight completely. He gets help to write to the DWP and notify the change. He is sent a new assessment questionnaire, which he completes with the help of a local advice centre. He includes a copy of his certificate of visual impairment. His award is changed to the enhanced rate daily living component and mobility component.

3. Have you been overpaid?

If you are paid more personal independence payment than you are entitled to, the Department for Work and Pensions (DWP) considers this to be an 'overpayment', and you may have to pay the money back.

You may have been overpaid if:

- you gave the wrong information when you claimed
- you were late reporting a change in your circumstances
- the DWP did not act on the information you gave straight away

If the DWP thinks you have been overpaid because you have deliberately not reported a relevant change in your circumstances, you may be considered to have acted fraudulently. This could lead to a criminal conviction or a penalty, and your personal independence payment could be suspended for a set period. You should therefore report immediately any change in your circumstances that might affect your entitlement. If you are not certain whether a change in your circumstances is relevant, you should report it.

If you have been told you have been overpaid, get specialist advice from a citizens advice bureau or welfare rights service.

Do you have to pay the money back?

You do not have to pay back an overpayment of personal independence payment unless it arose because you:

- did not tell the Department for Work and Pensions (DWP) something that you need to report
- made a statement to the DWP that was untrue

If either of the above apply, the overpayment can be recovered from you, even if your mistake was not deliberate.

You can challenge the decision that you have been overpaid and the decision to recover the overpayment. You should ask for a mandatory reconsideration and then if necessary appeal to a tribunal. You should also check that the amount of the overpayment is correct.

The DWP usually recovers overpayments through deductions from your ongoing award of personal independence payment, or by reducing the amount of any arrears it may owe you. Overpayments can also be recovered by making deductions from your other benefits. Ask the DWP to waive recovery of the overpayment if this is causing you hardship.

Overpayments can be complicated and confusing, and the consequences can be serious, so you should always get advice from, for example, a citizens advice bureau or other welfare rights service.

Further information

CPAG produces another guide in this series called *Winning your benefit appeal: What you need to know.*

CPAG's *Welfare Benefits and Tax Credits Handbook* contains detailed information about challenging decisions and overpayments, with references to the legislation and the most important caselaw.

Ask CPAG online (www.cpag.org.uk/welfare-rights) has a section on disputing personal independence disability decisions.

On www.gov.uk there is *Advice for Decision Making,* which the Department for Work and Pensions has produced for its own staff. Chapters A3 to A6 are about revisions (called mandatory reconsiderations in this book), supersessions (the legal name for a new decision if your circumstances have changed) and appeals.

Information on how to complete Form SSCS1 is in the leaflet *How to Appeal Against a Decision Made by the Department for Work and Pensions* (SSCS1A), available on the HM Courts and Tribunals Service website at www.justice.gov.uk/forms/hmcts/sscs.

Chapter 8
People in special circumstances

This chapter covers:

1. Are you in hospital?

2. Are you are in a care home?

3. Are you in prison?

4. Are you terminally ill?

What you need to know

- Both the daily living component and the mobility component of personal independence payment can only be paid for a maximum of 28 days while you are in hospital or prison, unless you are under 18 when you go into hospital.

- The daily living component can only be paid for a maximum of 28 days while you are in a publicly funded care home. The mobility component is not affected.

- When calculating the 28-day time limit, different periods spent in hospital, prison or a care home can sometimes be linked.

- If you claim personal independence payment when you are in hospital, a care home or prison, you cannot be paid until you leave (unless you are under 18 and in hospital). If you are a care home resident, this only applies to the daily living component.

- If you have a terminal illness you automatically qualify for the daily living component of personal independence payment. Some of the other rules, and the way your claim is dealt with, are different.

1. Are you in hospital?

Your personal independence payment is affected if you are a hospital inpatient, unless you went into hospital before your 18th birthday and have been there ever since. If you were under 18 when you went into hospital, payment of your personal independence payment continues throughout that stay as a hospital in-patient, even if you turn 18 during your stay.

If you are 18 or over and entitled to personal independence payment when you go into hospital, your entitlement continues but payment stops after 28 days. The days you enter and leave hospital do not count. Payment can start again from the day you leave hospital.

If you are 18 or over and awarded personal independence payment while you are in hospital, you cannot be paid until you leave.

Box A
Are you a hospital patient?

- A 'hospital' can also include a 'similar institution' to a hospital. This is not defined in the regulations, but it could include a care home, clinic or rehabilitation unit where you are receiving NHS-funded treatment provided or supervised by qualified doctors, nurses or other healthcare professionals.

- You do not count as being in a hospital if you are terminally ill and in a hospice that is not an NHS hospital or similar institution.

- Personal independence payment is not affected if you are a private patient.

If the DWP has treated you as a hospital patient, but you think you should have been treated as being in a care home (in which case, payment of your mobility component is unaffected), you should get advice. You may be able to challenge this decision.

Both the daily living component and mobility component are affected if you are 18 or over and go into hospital. If the DWP pays your mobility component directly to Motability to enable you to hire a car or wheelchair or buy one on hire purchase, payments will also stop after 28 days. You then have 28 days in which to return the car or wheelchair. This 28-day period may be extended by negotiation with Motability.

Definition of hospital

Jack is 42. He has been in hospital since late 2015. He is moved from a long-stay hospital into a nursing home where he receives medical treatment from staff based at the home. The NHS funds the treatment and the costs of his board and accommodation. He is entitled to both components of personal independence payment, but his payments stopped after he had been in hospital for 28 days. The Department for Work and Pensions decides that he is now in a 'similar institution' to a hospital and so his personal independence payment is still not payable.

Have you had more than one stay in hospital?

If you are 18 or over, different stays in hospital which are separated by 28 days or less are linked together when working out whether you have been in hospital for 28 days, after which time your payment stops. So, for example, if you were paid personal independence payment for 14 days while in hospital and you then go home for 20 days, you are paid during these 20 days, and for the first 14 days after you return to hospital.

Periods you spend in a care home or prison also link with periods you spend in hospital, provided they are separated by 28 days or less. This means that if you have already been paid the daily living component of personal independence payment for 28 days while in a care home and you go straight into hospital, you do not receive any further payment while in hospital if you are 18 or over. If you were getting the mobility component in the care home, it continues to be paid for the first 28 days you are a hospital patient.

EXAMPLES

The linking rules

Beatrice is 23. She is entitled to both components of personal independence payment. She goes into hospital on 1 July for an operation and is discharged on 15 July. Her personal independence payment is not affected because she has only been a patient for 13 days (the days she enters and leaves hospital do not count).

On 30 July, she goes back into hospital for further treatment and is discharged again on 30 August.

There are 16 days between Beatrice's two hospital stays, so the days she spends in hospital are linked together. She has already received personal independence payment for 13 days, so she can only be paid for a further 15 days, starting on 31 July. Her payments therefore stop from 15 August to 29 August.

Samir is resident in a care home. His daily living component of personal independence payment stopped after 28 days, but he still gets the mobility component. He goes into hospital for treatment. He cannot be paid the daily living component, but his mobility component continues to be paid for 28 days while he is in hospital.

2. Are you in a care home?

The daily living component of personal independence payment is affected if you are resident in a care home that provides nursing or personal care, and any of the costs of your accommodation, board and personal care are paid for out of public funds.

If you are entitled to the daily living component of personal independence payment when you go into a care home, your entitlement continues, but payment stops after you have been resident for 28 days. The days you enter and leave the home do not count. Payment can start again from the day you leave the home.

If you are awarded the daily living component while you are resident in a care home, it cannot be paid until you leave.

The mobility component of personal independence payment is not affected if you are in a care home, regardless of how long you stay there.

You do not count as being in a care home if you have a terminal illness and you are in a hospice, provided this is not an NHS hospital or 'similar institution'. In these circumstances, your personal independence payment is unaffected.

Box B
Paying for a care home

- The daily living component of personal independence payment only stops being paid if your accommodation, board and personal care are partly or wholly paid for by public funds under specified legislation. This mainly applies to local authority funding for disabled people. It does not include any social security benefits you may get. It does not matter whether it is a private or local authority care home – the important question is whether the local authority funds your place.

- If you are paying the full cost of your home and care yourself, or with the help of another person or a charity (known as 'self-funding'), you continue to be paid the daily living component. This also applies if a local authority is temporarily funding your placement while you sell your property, provided you are liable and able to repay the local authority when your property is sold (this is known as 'retrospective self-funding', but does not usually apply for the first 12 weeks you are permanently resident in a care home). The Department for Work and Pensions (DWP) may suspend payment of your daily living component while enquiries are made about whether you are self-funding. Once this is established, payments should resume and arrears paid to you.

Also, you may not count as being in a care home if you are receiving a significant amount of nursing or medical care in the home, so that your placement is (or should be) fully funded by the NHS. In these circumstances you count as being in a similar institution to a hospital and the rules on hospital patients apply.

EXAMPLES

Self-funding

William is entitled to the daily living component of personal independence payment. He is resident in a local authority care home. The costs are fully paid by a combination of his social security benefits, a charitable payment and his brother. His daily living component remains payable to him because he is 'self-funding'.

Hannah receives the daily living component of personal independence payment when she permanently moves into a care home. She owns a property which she intends to sell. Her local authority ignores the value of the property for 12 weeks and fully funds her placement.

Her daily living component stops being paid after she has been resident in the home for 28 days.

After 12 weeks, she has still not sold her property. The local authority can no longer ignore its value, but agrees to continue funding until it is sold, on the basis that Hannah will repay the local authority when the property is sold. During this period, she counts as 'self-funding' and the daily living component can be paid again.

Once the property is sold, Hannah continues to be self-funding until her savings fall below the level which entitles her to local authority funding again. When this happens, her daily living component will stop being paid.

It is not always clear whether you are receiving public funding under the specified legislation or whether you are self-funding. The DWP sometimes makes incorrect decisions based on inaccurate or unclear information provided by local authorities and care providers. If you think the DWP may have incorrectly stopped your daily living component, you should seek advice about challenging the decision.

What CPAG says

The rules when you are in hospital or residential care

CPAG is concerned that the rules on payment of personal independence payment, particularly of the daily living component, are too complex. It is often unclear whether you are resident in a care home or a 'similar institution' to a hospital. It can be hard to tell whether a place in a care home is being funded under the relevant legislation or whether you are self-funding, and decisions are sometimes wrongly made on the basis of unclear or inaccurate information. The linking rules for separate stays in hospital and care homes are also too complicated for most people to understand. They are likely to result in payments stopping and starting, with inevitable delays in payments being restored, causing hardship and distress to vulnerable people.

Have you had more than one stay in a care home?

Different stays in a care home separated by 28 days or less link together when working out whether you have been in a care home for 28 days, after which your daily living component stops.

So, for example, if you were paid the daily living component of personal independence payment for 25 days while you were resident in a care home and then you leave the home for 10 days, you are paid during these 10 days, and for the first three days after you return to the home.

Periods spent in prison or hospital (if you were 18 or over when you went into hospital) also link with periods spent in a care home, if they are separated by 28 days or less. This means that if you have already been paid the daily living component for 28 days while you were in hospital and you then go straight into a care home, you do not receive any further payment while you remain in the care home (unless you are 'self-funding'). If you go in and out of residential care, you may want to plan the timing to maximise payment of your daily living component.

EXAMPLES

Linking periods

Helen is 64. She has been in hospital for several weeks and her personal independence payment has stopped being paid. She then moves permanently into a care home, paid for by her local authority. The daily living component is not payable because her stays in hospital and the care home are linked as they are separated by 28 days or less.

Tom spends periods in and out of residential care, funded by the local authority. He is entitled to the daily living component of personal independence payment. If he goes into a care home on Sunday and returns home the following Friday, he counts as being resident in the home for four days (the days he enters and leaves do not count). He can repeat this pattern for seven weeks before he counts as being resident in the home for 28 days, when his payments will stop. If he goes home again, his payments will resume. If he spends at least 28 days at home, he continues to be paid for a further 28 days when he goes back into the care home.

---

3. Are you are in prison?

Your personal independence payment is affected if you are in prison or detained in legal custody.

- If you are entitled to personal independence payment when you enter prison, your entitlement continues, but payment stops after you have been in prison for 28 days. The days you enter prison and are released do not count. Payment can start again from the day you are released.

- If you are awarded personal independence payment while you are in prison, you cannot be paid while you remain in prison.

Box C
Are you in prison?

- You do not count as being in prison or legal custody if you are on bail, or released on parole, temporary licence or under a home detention curfew (electronic tagging).

- You do not count as being in prison or legal custody if you are detained in a hospital or similar institution after criminal proceedings because of a mental disorder (but the hospital rules may apply), unless you have been detained under specified mental health legislation.

Both the daily living and mobility components are affected if you are in prison.

Different periods spent in prison that are separated by a year or less link together when calculating the 28-day period during which you can continue to get personal independence payment while you are in prison. Periods spent in a care home or hospital (if you are 18 or over when you go into hospital) also link with periods spent in prison, provided they are separated by 28 days or less.

EXAMPLE

Linking periods

George is entitled to personal independence payment when he is taken into legal custody. He continues to be paid for 28 days, after which it stops. A month later, he is released on bail and his personal independence payment is paid again. Five months later, following a trial, he is imprisoned again. As this is within a year of his previous detention, payment of his personal independence payment stops again the day after he goes to prison.

4. Are you terminally ill?

If you are 'terminally ill', special rules apply to make it easier for you to qualify for personal independence payment.

What the law says

Terminal illness

- You are terminally ill if you have a progressive disease and death from that disease can reasonably be expected within six months.

- For the special rules to apply, you (or the person acting for you) must notify the Department for Work and Pensions that you are terminally ill.

Section 82 Welfare Reform Act 2012

What are the special rules?

If you are 'terminally ill', you automatically qualify for the daily living component of personal independence payment at the enhanced rate. It does not matter whether you currently have any problems with daily living activities or for how long you have been unwell. You do not have to wait three months to qualify.

You must still score at least eight points for the two mobility activities to get the mobility component of personal independence payment if you are terminally ill, but it does not matter how long your mobility needs have lasted or are expected to last. You do not have to have met the assessment criteria for three months before you qualify for the mobility component.

If you are terminally ill, you do not have to have been in Great Britain for two of the last three years to qualify for personal independence payment. You must still satisfy other residence tests.

Terminal illness

Camille had breast cancer which was thought to be in remission. However, she has just been told that the cancer has spread and caused a brain tumour, and that she probably only has a few months to live. Other than severe headaches some mornings, she currently has no symptoms that affect her ability to undertake the daily living activities in the personal independence payment assessment. She claims personal independence payment, and is awarded the daily living component at the enhanced rate from the date of her claim.

How do you claim?

If you are 'terminally ill', you, or someone on your behalf, can make a claim for personal independence payment either by telephone or by using a claim form. Someone else can claim for you, with or without your knowledge or permission. The claim itself is slightly different, as you are also asked questions about mobility problems caused by your condition.

You (or the person claiming for you) should get Form DS1500, confirming that you are terminally ill, from your GP, nurse or consultant. Send this to the Department for Work and Pensions (DWP), either when you make your claim, or as soon as possible after. Do not delay making your claim because you are waiting for the form – you can send it later.

The DWP informs you that a claim has been made, but does not refer to your having a terminal illness. If you are claiming on behalf of someone else, you should therefore inform her/him that a claim for personal independence payment has been made.

Instead of a questionnaire and consultation, a different assessment process is normally used if you are terminally ill. The DWP sends your claim information and the DS1500 form to the company carrying out the assessment. A healthcare professional then provides advice to the DWP about whether you meet the definition of terminal illness, and whether it is likely that you have mobility difficulties. This process allows the decision on your claim to be made more quickly.

EXAMPLE

Claims on the grounds of terminal illness

Brian has just been diagnosed with a terminal illness. He is obviously very upset and is struggling to cope. His wife Nina finds out about personal independence payment and claims by telephone on his behalf. She explains that her husband is terminally ill and gives his basic details. She is asked about his mobility needs and she explains that Brian gets breathless after walking just a few metres, and that this is the reason why he first went to the doctor. She sends Form DS1500 to the DWP, and explains to Brian that she has claimed some extra money for him. Two weeks later, Brian is awarded the daily living component and the mobility component of personal independence payment for three years. The letter explaining this does not mention the fact that he is terminally ill.

An award of personal independence payment on the basis of terminal illness is normally made for three years. If, during this time, you are told that your death can no longer be reasonably expected within six months, you should report this as a change in your circumstances. This is because you no longer meet the definition of 'terminal illness' and must be reassessed under the usual rules.

If you do not agree with a decision about your entitlement to personal independence payment, you can challenge it in the normal way (explained in Chapter 7). Someone who has claimed personal independence payment on your behalf without your knowledge can also request a 'mandatory reconsideration' and appeal without your knowledge.

Chapter 9
Personal independence payment and other benefits

This chapter covers:

1. Means-tested benefits
2. Other benefits
3. The benefit cap
4. Other financial help
5. Motability

What you need to know

- If you get personal independence payment, you may be entitled to an extra amount in any of your 'means-tested' benefits.

- Personal independence payment does not affect your entitlement to most 'non-means-tested' benefits.

- Getting personal independence payment means you are exempt from the 'benefit cap'.

- Your carer can claim carer's allowance if you get the daily living component. This can affect your benefits, so get advice first.

- If you get personal independence payment, you qualify for a 'Christmas bonus' and you may also qualify for parking or travel concessions.

- If you get the enhanced rate mobility component, the Motability scheme can help you hire or buy a car. You are also exempt from road tax (you get a 50 per cent reduction if you get the standard rate).

1. Means-tested benefits

'Means-tested benefits' are based on the amount of income and capital (such as savings) you have. They are:

- income support
- income-based jobseeker's allowance
- income-related employment and support allowance
- universal credit
- pension credit
- housing benefit
- child tax credit
- working tax credit

Each of these benefits has its own set of qualifying conditions based on your personal circumstances, such as whether you are unemployed, too sick to work, or if you need help to pay for your rent.

Personal independence payment is not counted as income when working out whether you are entitled to any of the above means-tested benefits, and it does not reduce how much benefit you get.

Can you get an extra amount?

If you get personal independence payment, you may qualify for an extra amount in your means-tested benefit, such as a 'premium' in income support, income-based jobseeker's allowance, income-related employment and support allowance and housing benefit, an 'additional amount' in pension credit, or an 'element' in universal credit or tax credits.

- If you are entitled to any amount of personal independence payment, you qualify for a 'disability premium' in income support and income-based jobseeker's allowance. You qualify for a disability premium in housing benefit if you are under the qualifying age for pension credit (this is the same age for men and women, but is based on the age when women can get retirement pension). There is no disability premium in employment and support allowance.

- If you are paid the enhanced rate daily living component, you qualify for an 'enhanced disability premium' in income support, income-based jobseeker's allowance, income-related employment and support allowance and housing benefit.

- If you are entitled to either rate of the daily living component, you qualify for a 'severe disability premium' in income support, income-based jobseeker's allowance, income-related employment and support allowance and housing benefit, provided you meet other qualifying conditions.

- If you are entitled to either rate of the daily living component, you qualify for a 'severe disability additional amount' in your pension credit, provided you meet other qualifying conditions.

- If you are entitled to any amount of personal independence payment and are over the qualifying age for pension credit, you qualify for a 'limited capability for work element' in your universal credit.

- If you are entitled to the enhanced rate daily living component and are over the qualifying age for pension credit, you qualify for a 'limited capability for work and work-related activity element' in your universal credit.

- If you are entitled to any amount of personal independence payment, you qualify for a 'disabled worker element' in working tax credit, provided you work 16 or more hours a week and meet an extra disability test.

- If you or your partner are entitled to the enhanced rate daily living component, you qualify for the 'severe disability element' in working tax credit. This can be paid in addition to the disabled worker element if you qualify for both.

If you are a student and you get personal independence payment, you can claim income-related employment and support allowance, provided you meet the other qualifying conditions. If you are a full-time student getting personal independence payment in an area where you must instead claim universal credit, you must also meet extra conditions to qualify.

If you or your partner are entitled to the daily living component of personal independence payment, no 'non-dependant deductions' are made from any help with your rent or mortgage you might get through income support, income-based jobseeker's allowance, income-related employment and support allowance, housing benefit, pension credit or universal credit. A 'non-dependant deduction' (known as a 'housing costs contribution' for universal credit) is an amount that is normally deducted from your means-tested benefit if you have an adult living with you who is not your partner. For universal credit only, no deduction is made from the housing costs of someone you live with due to your presence if you are entitled to the daily living component of personal independence payment.

Does your child get personal independence payment?

If you have a child who is 16 or over who gets personal independence payment and still counts as part of your household, you qualify for:

- a 'disabled child premium' in your housing benefit (if s/he gets the enhanced rate daily living component, you also qualify for an 'enhanced disability premium')
- a 'disabled child addition' in your universal credit (paid at a higher rate if s/he is entitled to the enhanced rate daily living component)
- an extra 'disabled child element' in your child tax credit (if s/he is entitled to the enhanced rate daily living component, you also qualify for a 'severely disabled child element')

2. Other benefits

Other, 'non-means-tested', benefits are not affected by any income and capital you have.

Personal independence payment can be paid in addition to most non-means-tested benefits, such as:

- contribution-based jobseeker's allowance
- contributory employment and support allowance

- carer's allowance
- bereavement benefits
- child benefit
- statutory maternity, paternity and adoption pay
- statutory sick pay
- maternity allowance
- retirement pension
- industrial injuries disablement benefit

Some non-means-tested benefits cannot be paid at the same time as personal independence payment. These are:

- disability living allowance
- attendance allowance
- constant attendance allowance (this could be paid as part of your industrial injuries benefit or war pension, and 'overlaps' with the daily living component)
- war pensioners' mobility supplement payable under the war pensions scheme, or grants for the use of a vehicle from the NHS (these 'overlap' with the mobility component)

Carer's allowance

Carer's allowance is a benefit for people who provide care for 35 hours or more a week to someone who is sick or disabled. If you get paid either rate of the daily living component of personal independence payment and someone regularly cares for you, s/he can claim carer's allowance, provided s/he meets the other qualifying conditions.

However, if you are entitled to a 'means-tested' benefit, you could lose money if someone claims carer's allowance for looking after you. This is because you may lose the additional 'severe disability premium' included in your benefit. The rules are complicated, so get advice before someone claims carer's allowance for looking after you.

3. The benefit cap

There is sometimes a limit on the total annual amount of benefits that you can receive if you are under the 'qualifying age for pension credit'. This is known as the 'benefit cap'. The limits are:

- £26,000 a year (£500 a week, or £2,167 a month) for couples (with or without children) or lone parents
- £18,200 a year (£350 a week, or £1,517 a month) for single adults who do not have children living with them

If the total amount of certain benefits that you get is more than the limits above, your housing benefit or universal credit is reduced.

From autumn 2016, the benefit cap will reduce to £23,000 a year for couples and claimants with children living in Greater London, £20,000 for couples and claimants with children living outside Greater London, £15,410 for single claimants living in Greater London and £13,400 for single claimants living elsewhere. This may be introduced in different areas at different times.

Personal independence payment is not one of the specified benefits included in the cap. If you, your partner or child get personal independence payment, you are exempt from the benefit cap. This exemption still applies if you are entitled to personal independence payment, but it is not payable because you are in hospital or a care home. There are other exemptions too, so seek expert advice if you or your family are affected by the beneift cap.

Once the reduced benefit cap applies, your carer will also be exempt from the benefit cap if s/he is entitled to carer's allowance.

4. Other financial help

You qualify for a 'Christmas bonus' if you are entitled to personal independence payment. This is currently £10.

If you are entitled to the mobility component of personal independence payment, you may qualify for a blue badge for parking concessions. You may also qualify for a concessionary travel card.

The rules are different in different areas. Contact your local authority for more information.

If you are entitled to the enhanced rate mobility component, you are exempt from road tax. If you are entitled to the standard rate, you can get a 50 per cent reduction in the cost of your road tax. Contact the Driver and Vehicle Licensing Agency (DVLA) for more information.

5. Motability

Motability is a scheme to help people with a long-term health condition or disability hire or buy a car, electric wheelchair or scooter. You can join the scheme if you receive the enhanced rate personal independence payment mobility component and your award has 12 months or more left to run.

If you do not drive, but you receive the enhanced rate mobility component, you can apply for a car as a passenger, nominating a maximum of two other people as your drivers.

Under the scheme, your mobility component is paid directly to Motability as a payment towards a vehicle. You may also have to make additional payments to Motability. The vehicle can be adapted to suit your needs.

Further information

Contact your local citizens advice bureau, local authority welfare rights service or other independent advice provider for more information about the benefits that you may qualify for if you are awarded personal independence payment.

Further information about road tax can be obtained from www.gov.uk/government/organisations/driver-and-vehicle-licensing-agency (telephone 0300 790 6802; textphone 0300 123 1279) and further information about the Motability scheme can be obtained from www.motability.co.uk (telephone 0300 456 4566; textphone 0300 037 0100).

Chapter 10
Transfers from disability living allowance

This chapter covers:

1. The transfer process

2. Can you choose to claim personal independence payment?

3. Who must claim personal independence payment?

4. How is your disability living allowance affected?

5. Will you be worse off?

What you need to know

- You cannot get disability living allowance and personal independence payment at the same time.

- At some point over the next couple of years, awards of disability living allowance for working-age people will stop and you must make a claim for personal independence payment instead.

- You can choose to claim personal independence payment instead of disability living allowance if you were under 65 on 8 April 2013.

- If you get disability living allowance and report a change in your condition, you are normally told to claim personal independence payment and your disability living allowance stops.

- People getting disability living allowance who were 65 or over on 8 April 2013 are not affected by personal independence payment and will continue to receive disability living allowance.

1. The transfer process

If you are currently getting disability living allowance, and you are 16 or over, you are affected by the transfer process when your disability living allowance award is coming to an end. The exception to this is that if you turned 65 on or before 8 April 2013, you do not have to transfer to personal independence payment and can continue to get disability living allowance.

The Department for Work and Pensions (DWP) will contact you to tell you that you must claim personal independence payment instead. If you do not respond, your disability living allowance will come to an end. It is not possible to know exactly when you will be transferred to personal independence payment if you have a long-term or indefinite award.

The government plans that by October 2017 everyone will have been contacted. By this date, around two million people getting disability living allowance will have been told to claim personal independence payment instead. Most people will transfer to personal independence payment, but many others may not be entitled.

What the law says

What you must be told

The DWP must write to you and:
- explain that your disability living allowance will end if you do not claim personal independence payment
- make it clear that you have 28 days in which to make the claim and state the date by when you must do so
- explain how you can claim personal independence payment

Regulation 7 The Personal Independence Payment (Transitional Provisions) Regulations 2013

You must be invited to claim personal independence payment in writing. The letter must tell you how to claim and that you must claim within 28 days or your disability living allowance will stop.

If you do not make a claim for personal independence payment within the 28-day period, your disability living allowance is suspended (the DWP can extend this time limit if it considers it reasonable to do so). The DWP writes to you again, giving you a further 28 days in which to claim. If you claim at this point, your disability living allowance is reinstated and you continue to receive it until a decision is made on your personal independence payment claim. If you do not make a claim for personal independence payment within the 28 days, your disability living allowance ends.

2. Can you choose to claim personal independence payment?

If you get disability living allowance, are aged at least 16 and were under 65 on 8 April 2013, you can choose to make a claim for personal independence payment.

However, many people who currently get disability living allowance will not qualify for personal independence payment or may receive a lower amount, so consider carefully whether you wish to make a claim. Get advice before doing so if you are unsure. If you begin the process of claiming personal independence payment, it cannot be stopped. Once you get a decision on your claim for personal independence payment, your disability living allowance stops, even if you are not awarded personal independence payment. Section 5 of this chapter explains some common situations in which you should think very carefully about whether to claim personal independence payment or not.

3. Who must claim personal independence payment?

If you are currently getting disability living allowance, you have to claim personal independence payment instead if:

- you report that there has been a change in your condition that could affect your disability living allowance award (unless you are in hospital and still getting paid your disability living allowance, or the change is that you go abroad)

- you reach the age of 16 (unless you are terminally ill at that date, or in hospital and still being paid your disability living allowance)
- your disability living allowance award is coming to an end

Even if you are not in one of these groups, you can be asked to claim personal independence payment at any time (unless you are not yet 16 or turned 65 on or before 8 April 2013). Check any letters that you get from the Department for Work and Pensions carefully to see if you are being told to claim personal independence payment.

Has your condition changed?

If you contact the Department for Work and Pensions (DWP) to report a change in your health condition or disability that could affect your disability living allowance award, or if you ask for a higher rate, the DWP invites you to claim personal independence payment. You should therefore think carefully before you contact the DWP. If you are unsure, get advice. Once you begin the process of claiming personal independence payment, it cannot be stopped.

If you contact the DWP to report another change in your circumstances, such as a change of address or because you have gone abroad for a period, or if you are in hospital and still getting paid your disability allowance, you are not automatically asked to claim personal independence payment. However, remember that you can be invited to claim personal independence payment at any point, and if you do not do so your disability living allowance will end.

Is your disability living allowance award coming to an end?

If you have a fixed-term award of disability living allowance (one that ends on a specific date), the Department for Work and Pensions (DWP) normally contacts you 20 weeks before your disability living allowance runs out and invites you to claim personal independence payment.

If you do not make a claim for personal independence payment when invited to do so, your disability living allowance award is ended. If you claim personal independence payment, your disability living allowance award is extended for as long as it takes the DWP to make a decision about your claim for personal independence payment.

Have you reached the age of 16?

Personal independence payment cannot be claimed by, or on behalf of, a child who is under 16. If you currently get disability living allowance for a child under 16, you continue to do so until s/he reaches her/his 16th birthday.

The Department for Work and Pensions (DWP) contacts you as s/he approaches this date, to find out if s/he wishes to make a claim for personal independence payment in her/his own right on reaching 16, or whether s/he still needs you to make the claim on her/his behalf (as her/his 'appointee'). The DWP should write to you when your child is aged 15 years and seven months and again when s/he is 15 years and 10 months.

If you are a young person who turns 16, the DWP normally writes to you (or your appointee if you have one), inviting you to claim personal independence payment.

If your disability living allowance award is due to end before you reach 16 and six months, it is automatically extended. If you make a claim for personal independence payment, you continue to get disability living allowance until either you reach 17, or a decision is made about your personal independence payment claim, whichever is sooner.

If you are getting disability living allowance under the special rules for people who are 'terminally ill', you continue to get disability living allowance beyond your 16th birthday until your award is due to end, and do not have to claim personal independence payment instead. If you are in hospital when you turn 16, you are not automatically asked to claim personal independence payment at that point.

EXAMPLES

16-year-olds

Daniel is age 16 and three months. When he turned 16, he responded to the DWP's letters and made a claim for personal independence payment. He returned the assessment questionnaire a few weeks ago and is still waiting for a consultation appointment. The DWP has not yet made a decision on his claim for personal independence payment, so Daniel continues to get disability living allowance.

Ethan had been getting disability living allowance since he was 11 because he has epilepsy. Three months ago, he turned 16. Both he and his parents received several letters from the DWP about claiming personal independence payment, which they ignored as his disability living allowance carried on being paid. They now notice that his disability living allowance has stopped. Ethan rings the DWP but is told that his disability living allowance has ended and he cannot get it back. Although Ethan can still make a claim for personal independence payment, his disability living allowance will not be reinstated while his claim is being considered.

Have you reached the age of 65?

If you are 65 or over and have never got disability living allowance or personal independence payment, you cannot get either and must claim attendance allowance instead.

If you reached 65 on or before 8 April 2013, you continue to get disability living allowance as usual. You are not transferred to personal independence payment. You can also qualify for different rates and get the care component for the first time.

However, if you turned 65 after 8 April 2013 and get disability living allowance, you are treated in the same way as a working-age claimant. This means that, at some point in the next few years, you will be invited to claim personal independence payment instead. You also have to claim personal independence payment if you report a change in your condition.

> **EXAMPLE**
>
> **65-year-olds**
>
> Fulmala gets the higher rate mobility component and the lowest rate care component of disability living allowance. She turned 65 in March 2013, so remains entitled to disability living allowance for as long as she meets the conditions of entitlement. She does not need to claim personal independence payment.
>
> Her husband Gurdeep also gets disability living allowance, but he turned 65 in June 2013. He is treated as a working-age claimant. Even though he wants to remain on disability living allowance, he will eventually be told that he must make a claim for personal independence payment.

4. How is your disability living allowance affected?

When you are told to make a claim for personal independence payment, you must do so. Chapter 3 describes how to claim personal independence payment.

What happens if you claim personal independence payment?

When you claim personal independence payment, your disability living allowance continues being paid until a decision is made about whether or not you are entitled to personal independence payment. When the decision is made, your disability living allowance normally stops 28 days after your next payday. If you are terminally ill, and your personal independence payment award is higher than your disability living allowance award was, your disability living allowance instead stops within one week of the decision awarding you personal independence payment.

You cannot challenge the decision to stop your disability living allowance. However, if you are refused personal independence payment, you can ask for a 'mandatory reconsideration' and then appeal. Chapter 7 has more details on challenging decisions.

If you are awarded personal independence payment, you are paid from the day after your disability living allowance stops.

EXAMPLES

If you claim personal independence payment

Hope has a fixed-term award of disability living allowance and gets the low rate care component. Her award is due to end in April 2017. She responds to the letter from the Department for Work and Pensions (DWP) telling her to claim personal independence payment, making her claim in December 2016. Her disability living allowance continues while her claim is dealt with. She is unable to attend a consultation appointment due to illness, and explains this to the DWP. The DWP accepts her explanation so her disability living allowance continues. On 23 May 2017, she is eventually awarded the personal independence payment standard rate daily living component. Her claim is not 'backdated' to the date she claimed personal independence payment. Instead, she receives two more payments of disability living allowance on 1 June and 28 June. Her entitlement to personal independence payment starts on 29 June.

Muriel gets the disability living allowance low rate mobility component and middle rate care component. She has an indefinite award, but chooses to claim personal independence payment in October 2016 as she hopes to get a higher amount. She is refused personal independence payment on 13 March 2017 and asks for a mandatory reconsideration. Her disability living allowance award ends. She gets two more payments of disability living allowance on 21 March and 18 April and then payment stops. If she is awarded personal independence payment, it will start from 19 April, the day after her disability living allowance stopped.

What happens if you do not claim personal independence payment?

If you do not make a claim for personal independence payment within the 28 days allowed, your disability living allowance is suspended. The Department for Work and Pensions (DWP) writes to you again, giving you another 28 days in which to claim. If you then claim personal independence payment, your disability living allowance is reinstated. This continues to be paid until a decision on your personal independence payment is made. If you do not make a claim for personal independence payment within the 28-day period, your entitlement to disability living allowance ends from the date it was suspended.

EXAMPLE

If you do not claim personal independence payment

Jake has a fixed-term award of disability living allowance that ends on 1 June 2017. On 12 February 2017, the DWP writes to him, telling him he must claim personal independence payment by 9 March. Jake has depression and does not respond to the letter. The DWP writes to him again on 12 March, telling him that payment of his disability living allowance has been suspended from 9 March and giving him a further 28 days to make a claim. Jake does not do this and his disability living allowance claim is terminated from 9 March.

If you contact the DWP to say you do not want to claim personal independence payment, your disability living allowance ends two weeks after your next payday.

If you want to claim personal independence payment, but think you need longer than 28 days, you should still try to contact the DWP within the 28-day period as you can then be given more time in which to complete the application. If you do not have all the details you need to make the claim (for example, you have lost your national insurance number), you should make the claim without it.

The DWP writes to you, giving you another month in which to supply the missing information.

What CPAG says

Getting help with letters

CPAG is aware of people who have lost their entitlement to disability living allowance before they realise they are in the transfer process. The most important thing is to check letters from the DWP to see what you need to do as soon as you get them, and to ask for help if you are unsure what you need to do.

What happens if your personal independence payment is refused?

If you claim personal independence payment, you should make sure that you comply with all the requests made by the Department for Work and Pensions (DWP), such as completing the assessment questionnaire and attending the consultation. If you do not, your claim could be refused. If this is the case, your disability living allowance also comes to an end two weeks after your next payday following the DWP's decision.

EXAMPLE

If personal independence payment is refused

Kevin has chronic fatigue syndrome and gets the low rates of both components of disability living allowance. When his fixed-term award is ending he is told to claim personal independence payment and he does so. However, he does not attend the consultation because when the invitation arrives he feels exhausted and cannot deal with the correspondence. His personal independence payment claim ends and his disability living allowance claim is terminated. He provides evidence of his ill health and the DWP accepts that he has a good reason for not attending the consultation and arranges another. Kevin is eventually awarded personal independence payment, and is paid from the day after his disability living allowance stopped.

If this happens, you can ask for a 'mandatory reconsideration' of the decision to refuse your personal independence payment – for example, if you had a 'good reason' for not sending back the questionnaire.

5. Will you be worse off?

Many people who currently get disability living allowance will not qualify for personal independence payment because the assessment criteria are different. One of the stated objectives of introducing personal independence payment was to save money. When personal independence payment was introduced, the government estimated that around half of all disability living allowance claimants would receive less money on personal independence payment, or get nothing at all.

If you do not have to make a claim, you should therefore think carefully before claiming personal independence payment or asking for a higher rate of disability living allowance, because you could lose your disability living allowance and not qualify for personal independence payment. You should consider the following points.

Do you currently get the low rate care component?

There is no equivalent of the disability living allowance low rate care component in personal independence payment. If you currently get this as part of your disability living allowance, you may be worse off when you have to claim personal independence payment. If you currently get paid the low rate care component for passing the 'cooking test' (you are assessed as being unable to prepare a cooked main meal for one person), you might find it difficult to score sufficient points under the preparing food activity alone to qualify for the daily living component of personal independence payment.

EXAMPLE

The cooking test

Lara currently gets the low rate disability living allowance care component on the basis that, on most days, she lacks the motivation to cook a main meal for herself and so just eats ready meals. When she is assessed for personal independence payment, she scores two points under descriptor 1(d) ('needs prompting to be able to either prepare or cook a simple meal') as she requires prompting to prepare the ingredients for a main meal for one. Unless she can score points for other activities, she will not get the daily living component of personal independence payment.

Do you need supervision?

You may have a general need to be supervised because, for instance, you have fits or seizures or because you are at risk of falls or self-neglect. If you are in this situation, you can get disability living allowance on the grounds that you need 'continual supervision throughout the day'. However, there is no equivalent way to qualify for the daily living component of personal independence payment. If you need to be supervised, you only score points if you can show that this is needed throughout the time you are doing one or more of the specific activities, such as preparing food or washing and bathing. If you have seizures on most days you should think about whether you actually need assistance from someone else to manage the activity 'safely'.

Do you get the higher rate mobility component because you are virtually unable to walk?

Many people currently get the disability living allowance higher rate mobility component because they are 'virtually unable to walk'. There is no precise definition of this. Personal independence payment is much more explicit about the distances you should be able to walk to qualify for the mobility component. If you can walk more than 20 metres as often as you need to, you could find that you only get the standard rate of the personal independence payment mobility component. If you are in this situation and have a Motability car paid for by your disability living allowance, you will no longer be able to access the scheme.

EXAMPLE

Problems walking

Muiread has chronic obstructive pulmonary disease and currently qualifies for the disability living allowance high rate mobility component, as she often experiences severe breathlessness and discomfort after she has walked about 50 metres and has to stop. How long she has to stop for and whether she can continue walking varies on different days. When assessed for personal independence payment, she scores eight points as the decision maker decides that she can walk more than 20 metres 'reliably'. This entitles her to the standard rate mobility component, the same amount as the disability living allowance low rate mobility component. Muiread should get help to think about how likely she is to succeed if she challenges this decision.

Do you need night-time care or supervision?

Unlike disability living allowance, the personal independence payment assessment does not distinguish between help you might need during the day and help you need at night.

If your disability living allowance is awarded partly on the basis that you need care or supervision during the night, you may struggle to qualify for personal independence payment for the same reasons. In particular, if you need supervision during the night to keep you safe, this will not necessarily mean you score any points in the personal independence payment assessment.

On the other hand, some people may benefit from the fact that there is no distinction between day and night. For example, if you are severely disabled and need a lot of help during the day, but have no night-time care needs, you can only qualify for the middle rate care component of disability living allowance. Under personal independence payment, your daytime needs may score you sufficient points to get the enhanced rate.

EXAMPLE

Significant daytime care needs

Neville has severe arthritis and needs help getting out of bed, washing, dressing, cooking, moving about indoors and taking his medication. He has no problems at night and so he currently gets the disability living allowance middle rate care component, even though his wife is his full-time carer. When he is assessed for personal independence payment, he scores more than 12 points and so gets the enhanced daily living component, equivalent to the disability living allowance high rate care component.

Can you follow journeys without help?

The high rate mobility component of disability living allowance is normally limited to those who have physical problems walking or severe sensory impairments. If your mobility difficulties are due to cognitive problems, you can usually only get the low rate of the disability living allowance mobility component. However, once you claim personal independence payment, you could qualify for the enhanced rate mobility component if you normally need someone else to help you to navigate the route of familiar journeys, regardless of whether this is due to physical or mental health problems.

However, if you have mental health problems and need reassurance and support when following unfamiliar journeys, you are likely only to be awarded the personal independence payment mobility component if you cannot go out at all most days or you get so anxious that you can no longer navigate without help. You should get advice about challenging a decision refusing you the mobility component if you have mental health problems.

Appendix 1

Glossary of terms

Activity
The personal independence payment assessment looks at how your health condition or disability affects your ability to carry out 12 everyday activities.

Additional amount
An extra amount of pension credit paid to people with additional needs, such as a disability or caring responsibilities.

Appointee
Someone, often a relative, authorised by the Department for Work and Pensions to claim and receive benefit on another person's behalf if that person is either under 16 or cannot claim for her/himself – for example, because of a learning disability.

Benefit cap
The maximum amount of social security benefits that you can receive. The cap does not apply if you, your partner or a child still included in your benefit claim are entitled to personal independence payment.

Capital
Includes savings, investments, certain lump-sum payments and property which is not your main home.

Care component
The part of disability living allowance paid if you need help looking after yourself or someone to keep an eye on you because of your disability or health problem.

Case manager
A member of staff employed by the Department for Work and Pensions who makes decisions on entitlement to personal independence payment.

Christmas bonus
An extra payment of £10 paid to people receiving certain benefits (including personal independence payment) in the week beginning on the first Monday in December.

Component
One of the two parts of a personal independence payment or disability living allowance award.

Cooking test
A test of whether you can cook a main meal for yourself that qualifies you for the disability living allowance low rate care component.

Daily living component
The part of personal independence payment paid if you have problems with daily living activities, or are terminally ill.

Descriptor
A statement describing your ability to carry out one of the specific daily living or mobility activities.

Disability premium
An extra amount of income support, income-based jobseeker's allowance and housing benefit paid to people getting personal independence payment or certain other benefits, or who are registered blind.

Disabled child addition
An extra amount of universal credit paid for a child or young person who gets disability living allowance or personal independence payment or is registered blind.

Disabled child element
An extra amount of child tax credit paid for a child or young person who gets disability living allowance or personal independence payment or is registered blind.

Disabled child premium
An extra amount of housing benefit paid for a child or young person who gets disability living allowance or personal independence payment or is registered blind.

Disabled worker element
An extra amount of working tax credit paid to someone with a disability.

Elements
Amounts for children, disability, caring responsibilities, housing and childcare that make up part of someone's maximum universal credit award.

Enhanced disability premium
An extra amount of income support, income-based jobseeker's allowance, employment and support allowance and housing benefit paid to people getting the personal independence payment enhanced rate daily living component or the disability living allowance high rate care component.

European Economic Area
The 28 European Union member states, plus Iceland, Norway and Liechtenstein. For benefit purposes, Switzerland is also treated as part of the European Economic Area.

Forward condition
The nine months in the future during which time you must meet the qualifying conditions for personal independence payment.

Habitually resident
Someone who has a settled intention to stay in the UK, and who has usually been living here for a period.

Healthcare professional
A doctor, nurse, paramedic, physiotherapist or occupational therapist who carries out assessments for personal independence payment.

Limited capability for work element
An extra amount of universal credit paid to people whose ability to work is limited because of illness or disability.

Limited capability for work-related activity element
An extra amount of universal credit paid to people who are too ill to prepare for work or have a severe disability.

Mandatory reconsideration
When you ask for the Department for Work and Pensions to change a decision on your personal independence payment claim.

Mandatory reconsideration notice
Notice sent by the Department for Work and Pensions after you make a mandatory reconsideration request, which is needed in order to appeal.

Means-tested benefit
A benefit that is only paid if your income and capital are low enough, and which also considers the circumstances of your partner.

Motability
A scheme that allows you be buy or lease a vehicle with your personal independence payment enhanced rate mobility component or disability living allowance high rate mobility component.

Mobility component
The part of disability living allowance or personal independence payment paid if you have mobility problems.

Non-dependant deductions
Deductions from your housing benefit or universal credit if certain other adults live with you.

Non-means-tested benefit
A benefit that is paid regardless of the amount of your income or capital.

Overpayment
An amount of benefit that is paid to you, but which is more than your entitlement and which you may be asked to repay.

Passporting
A term used to describe when entitlement to a particular benefit allows access to other benefits or sources of help.

Person subject to immigration control
Someone who requires leave to enter or remain in the UK but does not have it, or who has leave to remain but is prohibited from having recourse to public funds, or has leave to remain in the UK on the basis of a sponsorship agreement.

Premium
Extra amounts of benefit paid with means-tested benefits depending on your circumstances.

Qualifying age for pension credit
Linked to women's pension age, which is currently increasing and will reach 65 by 2018 and 66 in 2020.

Required period condition
The qualifying period for personal independence payment, normally three months before and nine months after the date of your claim.

Retrospective self-funding
A term used to describe when the local authority is temporarily funding your placement in a care home while you sell your property, after which you must repay the money.

Revision
A way that the Department for Work and Pensions can change a benefit decision. Normally referred to as 'mandatory reconsideration'.

Right to reside
A social security test, mainly affecting European Economic Area nationals, which must be satisfied in order to claim certain benefits (not including personal independence payment).

Self-funding
A term used to describe when you are paying the full cost of your placement in a care home yourself.

Severe disability additional amount
An extra amount of pension credit paid if you are getting the daily living component of personal independence payment (or attendance allowance or the disability living allowance middle or high rate care component) and satisfy certain other conditions.

Severe disability premium
An extra amount of means-tested benefits paid if you are getting the daily living component of personal independence payment (or attendance allowance or the disability living allowance middle or high rate care component) and satisfy certain other conditions.

Severly disabled child element
An extra amount of child tax credit paid for a child or young person who gets the disability living allowance high rate care component or the personal independence payment enhanced rate daily living component.

Similar institution
An institution which is similar to a hospital for the personal independence payment rules.

Supersession
A term used by the Department for Work and Pensions when it changes a benefit decision, usually as a result of a change in your circumstances.

Terminal illness
A progressive disease from which your death can reasonably be expected within six months.

Upper Tribunal
The independent judicial body that decides appeals against tribunal decisions on points of law. Its decisions are binding on the Department for Work and Pensions.

Appendix 2

Meaning of terms used in the descriptors

Aided
With:
(a) the use of an aid or appliance; or
(b) supervision, prompting or assistance.

Assistance
Physical intervention by another person and does not include speech.

Assistance dog
A dog trained to guide or assist a person with a sensory impairment.

Basic verbal information
Information in the claimant's native language conveyed verbally in a simple sentence.

Basic written information
Signs, symbols and dates written or printed standard size text in the claimant's native language.

Bathe
Includes getting into or out of an unadapted bath or shower.

Communication support
Support from a person trained or experienced in communicating with people with specific communication needs, including interpreting verbal information into a non-verbal form and vice versa.

Complex budgeting decisions
Decisions involving:
(a) calculating household and personal budgets;
(b) managing and paying bills; and
(c) planning future purchases.

Complex verbal information
Information in the claimant's native language conveyed verbally in either more than one sentence or one complicated sentence.

Complex written information
More than one sentence of written or printed standard size text in the claimant's native language.

Cook
Heat food at or above waist height.

Dress and undress
Includes putting on and taking off socks and shoes.

Engage socially
(a) interact with others in a contextually and socially appropriate manner;
(b) understand body language; and
(c) establish relationships.

Manage incontinence
Manage involuntary evacuation of the bowel or bladder, including use a collecting device or self-catheterisation, and clean oneself afterwards.

Manage medication or therapy
Take medication or undertake therapy, where a failure to do so is likely to result in a deterioration in the claimant's health.

Medication
Medication to be taken at home which is prescribed or recommended by a registered:
(a) doctor;
(b) nurse; or
(c) pharmacist.

Monitor health
(a) detect significant changes in claimant's health condition which are likely to lead to a deterioration in claimant's health; and
(b) take action advised by a:
(i) registered doctor;
(ii) registered nurse; or
(iii) health professional who is regulated by the Health Professions Council,
without which the claimant's health is likely to deteriorate.

Orientation aid
A specialist aid designed to assist disabled people to follow a route safely.

Prepare
In the context of food, means make food ready for cooking or eating.

Prompting
Reminding, encouraging or explaining by another person.

Psychological distress
Distress related to an enduring mental health condition or an intellectual or cognitive impairment.

Read
Includes read signs, symbols and words but does not include read Braille.

Simple budgeting decisions
Decisions involving:
(a) calculating the cost of goods; and
(b) calculating change required after a purchase.

Simple meal
A cooked one-course meal for one using fresh ingredients.

Social support
Support from a person trained or experienced in assisting people to engage in social situations.

Stand
Stand upright with at least one biological foot on the ground.

Supervision
The continuous presence of another person for the purpose of ensuring the claimant's safety.

Take nutrition
(a) cut food into pieces, convey food and drink to one's mouth and chew and swallow food and drink; or
(b) take nutrition by using a therapeutic source.

Therapeutic source
Parenteral or enteral tube feeding, using a rate-limiting device such as a delivery system or feed pump.

Therapy
Therapy to be undertaken at home which is prescribed or recommended by a:
(a) registered:
(i) doctor;
(ii) nurse; or
(iii) pharmacist; or
(b) health professional regulated by the Health Professions Council.

Toilet needs
(a) getting on and off an unadapted toilet;
(b) evacuating the bladder and bowel; and
(c) cleaning oneself afterwards.

Unaided
Without:
(a) the use of an aid or appliance; or
(b) supervision, prompting or assistance.

Schedule 1, Part 1 Social Security (Personal Independence Payment) Regulations 2013

Appendix 3

Personal independence payment legislation

Part 4 Welfare Reform Act 2012

The Personal Independence Payment (Transitional Provisions) Regulations 2013 No.387

The Social Security (Personal Independence Payment) Regulations 2013 No.377

The Universal Credit, Personal Independence Payment, Jobseeker's Allowance and Employment and Support Allowance (Claims and Payments) Regulations 2013 No.380

The Universal Credit, Personal Independence Payment, Jobseeker's Allowance and Employment and Support Allowance (Decisions and Appeals) Regulations 2013 No.381

You can find the legislation at www.legislation.gov.uk.

Official guidance

Guidance for personal independence payment decision makers at the Department for Work and Pensions is in *Advice for Decision Making*, available at www.gov.uk.

There is also information about personal independence payment at www.gov.uk, including a 'toolkit' for advisers and claimants. This has factsheets and sample forms and letters.

Guidance for health professionals is in the *Personal Independence Payment Assessment Guide*, which is also published at www.gov.uk.

Index